Regeneration & Co-Creation

Changing Change

Keith Humphrey

This book is dedicated to my wife Penny, with whom life, love and growth
are not just essential, but compulsory.

Published by Core Context Consulting Ltd

ISBN 978-0-9558449-0-4 Regeneration & Co-Creation

Printed in Spain by Jiménez Godoy, s.a.

Core Context Consulting Ltd, Maple House, Bayshill Road, Cheltenham GL50 3AW T: +44 (0)870 420 3161 F: +44 (0)870 420 3162 E: khumphrey@corecontext.co.uk www.corecontext.co.uk

About the Author

Keith has been an advisor in the field of Individual Organisational and Strategy development for over thirty years. His work includes organisational design, advising boards on people strategy, designing strategic processes, consulting on board and team effectiveness and designing and implementing business development strategies and processes. He has created and delivered transformational leadership programmes; helped consultants and consulting organisations regenerate themselves and their offerings to clients; developed and facilitated organisational culture change programmes; and coached key individuals to become the best leaders they can be.

Keith is a principal partner in Core Context Consulting and has worked with high profile clients in many industry sectors on complex projects all over the world. He tends to have long term engagements, moving in and out of a handful of organisations over long periods of time.

Recent and ongoing clients include Citic Prudential, The Coca Cola Company, Coca Cola Enterprises, Northern Ireland Civil service, PwC (UK, Eurofirms, A7), and Wincanton Logistics.

Apart from his wife and his work, Keith is also passionate about tennis – playing, sponsoring, spectating; Food – shopping, cooking and eating; Wine – drinking and occasionally spilling.

About the Conceptual Artist – Karen Mortimore

Karen's interests and passion lie in expressing inner meaning in the external world.
Using an eclectic choice of media she loves bringing ideas to vibrant life

About this book

My intention is that the identity of this book should stand out in four significant ways.

It has a strong design signature. All of the images apart from one, which was co-created with a client, are new and have been created especially to add layers of meaning to this book. There is a dynamic mixture of narrative, signs, slogans, and symbols which I hope will make it a pleasure to read and share with others.

There are no case studies, I find case studies quickly become stale and at best are self serving and at worst embarrasing to the 'owners' of the case. All of my examples, and there are many of them, are drawn from my accumulated understanding of how individuals and organisations excel and disappoint. I hope that you will find your own particular examples springing quickly to mind.

This book is about all organisations not just businesses. Any group of people who band together with common purpose can and should embed continuous regeneration in their fabric. Continents, Regions, Religions, Governments, NGO's, Corner Shops, Families and Sports Teams all need to continuously rebase themselves, their Identity, Significance, and Competence in the light of their current and predicted future context. So even though the examples used in the book, stem from commercial organisations, the principles of regeneration hold true for all organisations.

The book is very optimistic. It is always amazing, given the vast possibilities for failure and despair that individuals and organisations continue to flourish, satisfy and bring great joy. The book does deal with the sometimes acute neurotic shadow that can pervade individuals and organisations; however, regeneration is an optimistic, practical antidote to dealing with degeneration, draining the stagnant pools and re-oxygising the environment.

You can read this book in five minutes by reading the section heading pages. These are on pages 8, 34, 78 and 112. This will help you dive into the book but we hope you stay in and enjoy swimming.

Contents

❊ see thank yous page 162

REGENERATION & CO-CREATION
Flourishing Over Time

Organisations are social phenomena, nothing happens without people talking and listening to each other in purposeful conversations.

Organisations have stakeholders who are all of those parties who need the organisation to be successful over time. These needs are often unsatisfied because of breakdowns in stakeholder conversations. Stakeholders either don't understand each others' needs, aren't organised to meet the current need or are doing a good enough job for now, but not the future.

In order to keep recreating a sustainable, profitable future an organisation must build the capacity to regenerate, rebase, revivify. This cannot just be done at a Competence level by changing the cast of leadership characters or tuning skills and processes.

Clarity about Identity, who are we in our current context and Significance, what we aspire to be in the future are essential to fuel and guide Competence. Taking periodic pauses to Regenerate, Identity, Significance and Competence through a co-creative process leads to an organisation which is always relevant, slightly ahead of its time and meeting stakeholder needs.

When organisations lose sight of their stakeholders needs and therefore their reason to exist and believe, they are out of touch with current reality. If this is continuous they begin to slide into a Degenerative cycle of Anomie, losing their commercial, social and ethical compass. Notoriety, where they become famous for continuing not to reach their dubiously based targets and Mediocrity, where their products and services infuriate or turn away their stakeholders.

CO-CREATION
ENSURES
SUSTAINABILITY

REGENERATE
COMPETENCE
TO FULFIL IDENTITY
+ REACH SIGNIFICANCE

COMPETENCE

IDENTITY

SIGNIFICANCE

LEGACY
FUNDEMENTAL
CHANGE ENRICHING
FUTURE GENERATIONS

REVIVIFYING,
NOT JUST
SHAKING THE
CORPSE

(EVO)

F*REWORKS

+ QUIET ENDEAVOUR

ALWAYS RELEVANT
ALWAYS SLIGHTLY
AHEAD OF ITS TIME

CLEAR IDENTITY - CREATES → LOVE
CLEAR SIGNIFICANCE - CREATES → POWER
CLEAR COMPETENCE - CREATES → RESPECT

STAKEHOLDERS

UNIVERSE
ALL PARTIES WITH A VESTED INTEREST IN THE LONG TERM FUTURE OF THE ORGANISATION

ANOMIE
NOTORIETY
MEDIOCRITY

REVOLUTIONS
SEEDED BY MANY SMALL
EVOLUTIONARY SHIFTS

ARE THE CLIMACTIC
PHASES OF EVOLUTION

THINGS ONLY GET DONE
WHEN THE RIGHT CONVERSATIONS
TAKE PLACE

REGENERATION & CO-CREATION
- FLOURISHING OVER TIME

Building
a Legacy

Sustainability
Flourishing Over Generations

Identity Significance
Competence

Regeneration -
A Positive Change Cycle

Leadership, Followership
and Co-Creation

Degeneration -
A Negative Change Cycle

Revolution
and Evolution

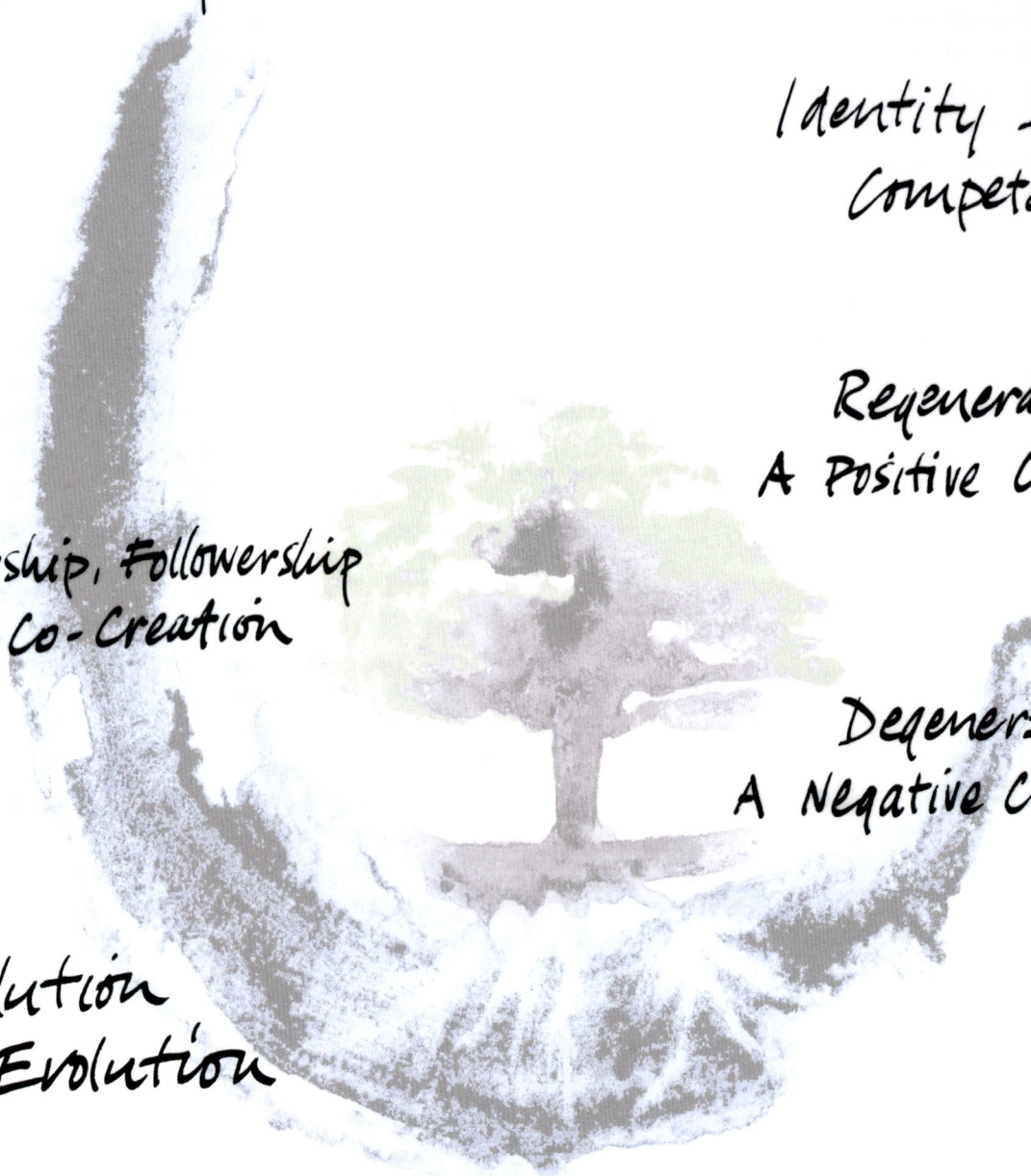

REGENERATION & CO-CREATION
Understanding and embedding positive change

Organisations are social phenomena. Things only get done when the right conversations take place. Productivity is stifled when people don't or can't talk and listen to each other. In a volatile environment it is essential for organisations to initiate and sustain new, more profound, conversations with their stakeholders - all those with a vested interest in the long-term future success of the enterprise. These stakeholder conversations are a catalyst to innovation. Enabling the **Regeneration** needed if organisations are to achieve the significant increases in productivity routinely expected of them by ever demanding stakeholders and necessary for them to flourish over generations.

Organisations always fail to match stakeholder needs on a consistent basis and therefore don't continually maximise and realise gains in productivity. This can be attributed to breakdowns in communication across one or more of their stakeholder conversations. This can lead to various outcomes, such as:

- Organisations and their leaders do not have a good grasp of what their stakeholders need from them. This can be as fundamental as a fashion retailer misjudging its customers' taste in clothes, or as complex as a financial services provider misreading conflicting regulatory trends.

- Organisations understand stakeholder needs, but their approach to meeting them has become outdated. Perhaps they have failed to update their channel or supplier strategy as more purchasing has gone on-line, or they have failed to take advantage of outsourcing opportunities ahead of their competitors.

- They make a reasonable day-to-day job of meeting stakeholder needs, but have no mechanism or culture for challenging themselves and driving improvement. Maybe rigid hierarchical management structures restrict positive change initiatives, or complacent leaders are failing to look beyond their own self aggrandisement or reward.

Sustainability flourishing over generations

An organisation's capacity to change, to adapt, is a prerequisite for its survival. The problem is that, all too often, leaders address their emerging external challenges by implementing a sequence of reactive, stop/start initiatives. Of necessity, these deal with surface issues and, as a result, they simply change the cast of leadership characters, or modify existing processes and procedures rather than addressing the long-term direction and values of the organisation. The longer this attitude persists, the more diluted, disenfranchised and disorientated the organisation's culture becomes.

The overarching goal of leadership is to build an organisation which satisfies its stakeholder's needs over the medium to long-term; to grow, to build, to shape a system that is always 'slightly ahead of its time'. There will always be a need for short term bursts of, sometimes seemingly contradictory activity. However, unless this activity is contextualised in a medium to long-term strategy, it will be received as disconnected actions which exploit the current circumstances, rather than build generational growth and sustainability. It is essential that short term and long term needs are addressed in parallel. Both are vital.

This shift from just an exploitative, short-term mindset - often tied to the leader's and some stakeholder's needs for speedy personal gratification (material and psychological) - to a sense of leadership in the service of building a sustainable organisation is fundamental to the way leadership is expressed. Building this long-term view means establishing trust, credibility and a co-creative mindset with a broad spectrum of stakeholders.

As the leader's work becomes more complex, full of paradox and the resulting dilemmas and contradictions, there is a need for a commercial, social and moral compass, for personal as well as corporate values to navigate toward a sustainable future.

In tough times, organisations can quickly lose touch with their instincts and values, their direction and their spirit. Because management teams commit to fire-fighting strategies, they fail to plan ahead. As a result, there is no legacy culture, no deep structure – and no sense of future. Leaders need to take time to understand their organisations, their relationship to their stakeholders and the sustainable interdependent futures which are possible for all of them.

One of the positive benefits of the upsurge in private equity ownership has been a move toward promoting active longer term value growth by rigorous reshaping of the organisation's potential rather than, organisations and their leaders being on the receiving end of the remorseless quarterly demands of public ownership, without the encouragement to rebase their organisations for future growth.

Instead of allowing short-term external developments to dictate organisational strategy – and inviting, in the process, an increasingly directionless 'management' philosophy to take root, organisations must be more far-sighted – addressing where they have come from and where they need to go. Organisations need to build on their existing strengths. Flexibility, innovation and resilience are all achievable goals. The key to sustainability is regeneration.

Revolution and Evolution

Organisations, groups and individuals are always changing. There is a spiralling, inter-weaving dance between what we do and the conditions under which we do things. Choosing to do a lot and choosing to do nothing both have the potential to provoke equally powerful consequences.

Change is internally and externally generated. Needs shift, evolve and sometimes completely transform. At the same time, the environment is in continual flux – setting new agendas and creating new needs.

External, contextual change has become an increasingly unpredictable influence on organisations. Global economic shifts are transforming the market. Ownership structures and all stages of the value chain are in evolution, from R&D and marketing to sales and procurement, irrespective of industry and location. Industry sector boundaries are becoming blurred. Regulatory pressures, including the drive to improved governance and enhanced transparency, are causing management agendas to be rewritten with a greater emphasis on personal and social responsibility. Global convergence and social and political volatility mean that competition and disruption can arrive quickly from unexpected quarters as new players seek to take advantage of the wider disequilibrium.

Typically, organisations and individuals react to changing landscapes by slightly changing themselves – correcting where they are going so they can still reach their previous objectives.

Organisations need to embrace the fact that **effective regenerative change** is about developing new ways of thinking and feeling that suit their long-term aspirations, as well as just adapting what they did in the past in an ad hoc, reactive way. Although these short term adjustments are vital they can never be enough.

Regenerative change is therefore both evolutionary and revolutionary. Revolution is only a climatic phase of an evolutionary process. Any revolution is seeded by many small evolutionary shifts in thinking, feeling and doing. Evolution contains many revolutionary points.

Leadership, Followership and Co-Creation

Regenerative change engages all stakeholders in a multi dimension dance or journey where all parties are leaders and followers; where conversations for co-creating the future are the responsibility of everyone. By definition all stakeholders have a legitimate right to be in the conversation and to have their needs met. However, different stakeholders needs will be in the foreground or background in terms of importance depending on where the enterprise is in its regenerative cycle.

Bringing a co-creative mindset to regeneration where joint agendas are created rather than where pre-determined views and demands are negotiated over, ensures that evolution and revolution happen in the pursuit of goals that meet all the stakeholders needs to build an organisation which will flourish over generations or appropriately die at the right time.

The foundations of regenerative change

Regenerative change is the continuous cycle through which we move between the states of **Identity** (who we are), **Significance** (the impact we aspire to) and **Competence** (what we do). At any one stage in a change pattern an organisation's identity may be in the foreground, with significance and competence both requiring attention in the background. This dynamic will shift as each of the three states assumes greatest prominence. But all three - identity, significance and competence - are interlinked. Change to one means change to the other two.

At any given moment leaders and their organisations are negotiating change from one state to another. Regeneration means rebasing, revivifying the organisation and the way it is led as opposed to just rebadging, 'shaking the corpse' or changing the cast of leaders.

To be fully effective the continuous cycle needs to engage individuals, teams, the organisation and its significant stakeholders in a co-creative process. Each element is interlinked, interdependent and in flux. Regeneration works best when all constituencies are aligned in their regenerative journey through identity, significance and competence.

All stakeholders are fundamentally linked because they have complementary sets of needs and wants which when satisfied ensure mutual survival and generational growth.

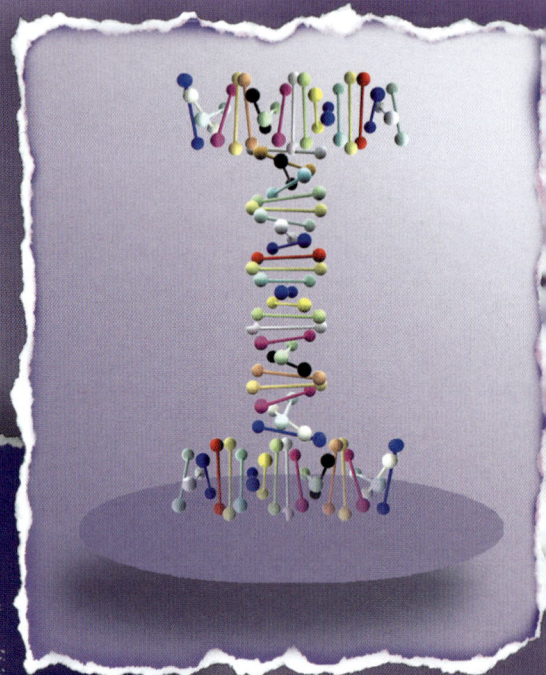

Identity - changes and remains the same

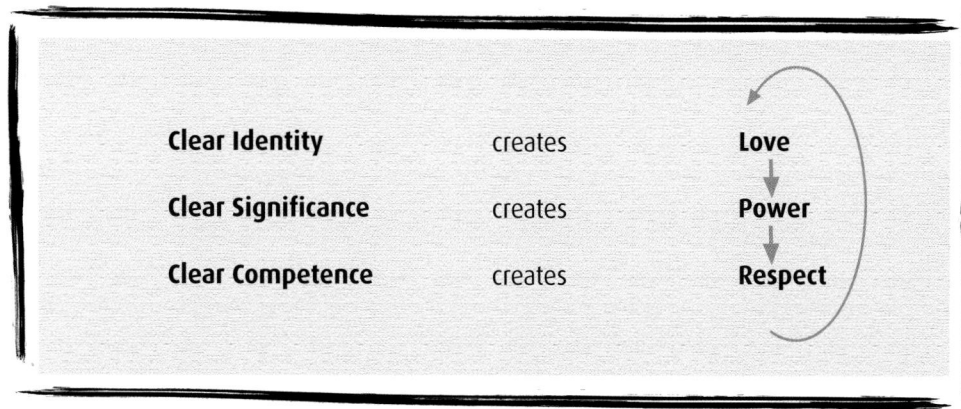

Clear Identity	creates	Love
Clear Significance	creates	Power
Clear Competence	creates	Respect

Identity

The basic human need for a sense of identity is a need to grow and be fully differentiated in that growth, to have the right degree of difference in order to stand out, along with the right degree of similarity; in order to be accepted. This acceptance is expressed and received as an emotional connection that stems from a blend of attractive differentiation and similarity that at its extreme is called Love. Individuals need the right degree of connection, consideration, regard, affection and love to flourish over time. Similarly, organisations need a compelling public identity or brand that is loved enough to continually attract financial and human capital to deliver on its organisational purpose. The optimum expression of identity is one where the degrees of similarity and difference are in a virtuous cycle where individuals and organisations needs are met with deeply reassuring yet striking different connections.

Significance

What we aspire to – when expressed clearly, sets out the amount of power we want to exert in the world, what impact we want to make and the fundamental differences we expect to accomplish. This expression of power and the potency of its application is a function of finding the sweet spot where what you really need is aligned with the epitome of what is possible. The integrative point where great challenge meets optimal opportunity galvanises motivation, thought and actions in a transformational expression of power. This integrative point is best found when a longer term mindset is brought to future possibilities, so the power you aspire to is seen over generations of possibility, rather than an attempt to regain control over what has just gone wrong or be in charge of a short term future agenda.

To be optimally powerful there needs to be a virtuous cycle between what is desirable and what is possible.

Competence

When what needs to be done is done in a manner which really satisfies the need, we create lasting Respect for our competence. There is a sense of acute satisfaction for both the executor and the receiver at a job marvellously done and a skill beautifully articulated. If the goods and the services provided are robustly rooted in the present and future needs of the consumer and the organising capacity that delivers them adds delight to the experience, a virtuous cycle is created. True competence is the capability of delivering the operating promise inherent in every transaction in a style which deepens the future relationship

Regeneration – a positive change cycle
This cycle must be ongoing. The alternative, stagnation, leaves individuals, teams, and organisations with

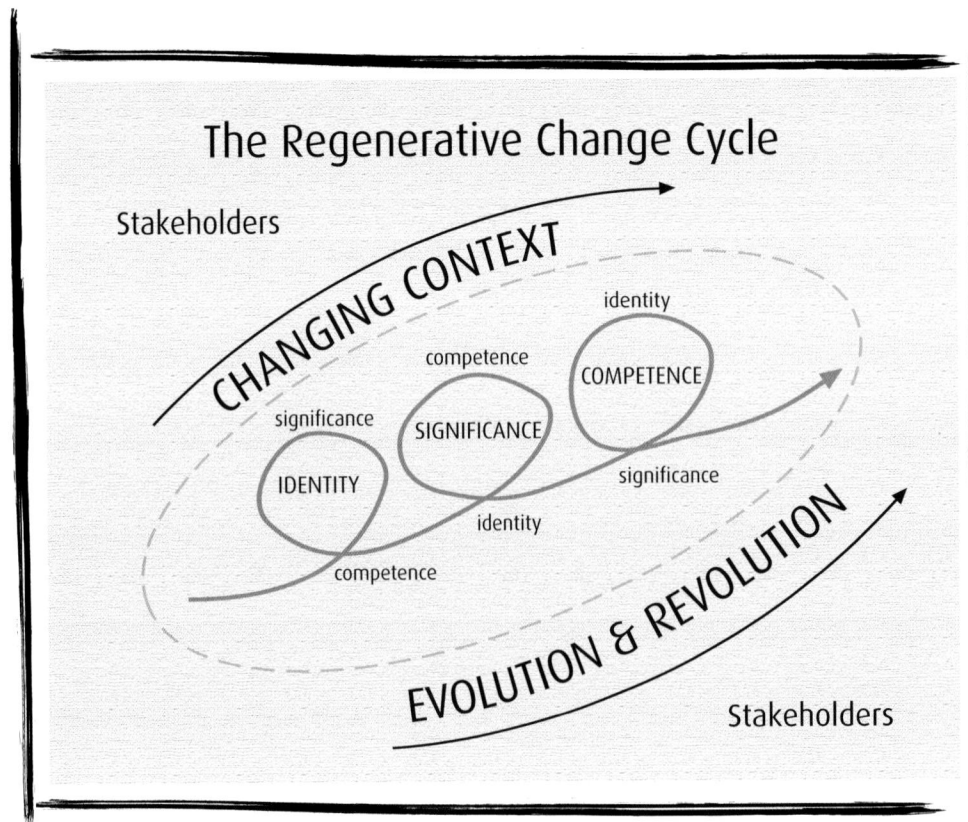

The Regenerative Change Cycle

Stakeholders

CHANGING CONTEXT

identity

competence

COMPETENCE

significance

SIGNIFICANCE

IDENTITY

significance

identity

competence

EVOLUTION & REVOLUTION

Stakeholders

'stuck' identities, 'stuck' significances and 'stuck' competencies. For example, where individuals are concerned, a leader with a stuck identity may be unable to adapt to a new post-merger organisational culture; with a stuck competence they might refuse to learn new relevant technical skills; and with a stuck significance, they may be overly willing to agree to limited strategic objectives instead of pushing towards challenging, more desirable futures. Individuals and organisations that are stuck are prone to entering a negative degenerative spiral where they become incompetent, badly goaled and with a shaky sense of what they exist to do.

Stuck organisations are the legitimate prey of private equity and other merger and take-over activity. These organisations are, at least, not living up to their potential. They may have lost their sense of self in their market, their brand may have less meaning and they are likely to have less sense of internal aligned common purpose. The services and products they are trying to sell will become less valued, replicable commodities of little interest to their stakeholders. They will be structured and behave in ways which have more to do with their residual history rather than their current and future needs for effectiveness.

INTER-LINKAGE OF IDENTITY, SIGNIFICANCE, COMPETENCE

When one aspect needs conspicuous work – be it identity, significance or competence – the remaining two will also require attention. If one is changed the other two must be realigned to coincide. This necessarily brings about changes to both the external and internal faces of the organisation and the dynamics of their stakeholders.

The Organisational Persona

External face

Brand —— Legacy —— Goods/Services

LOVE —— POWER —— RESPECT
IDENTITY   SIGNIFICANCE   COMPETENCE

Culture —— Prophecy —— Organising capacity

Internal face

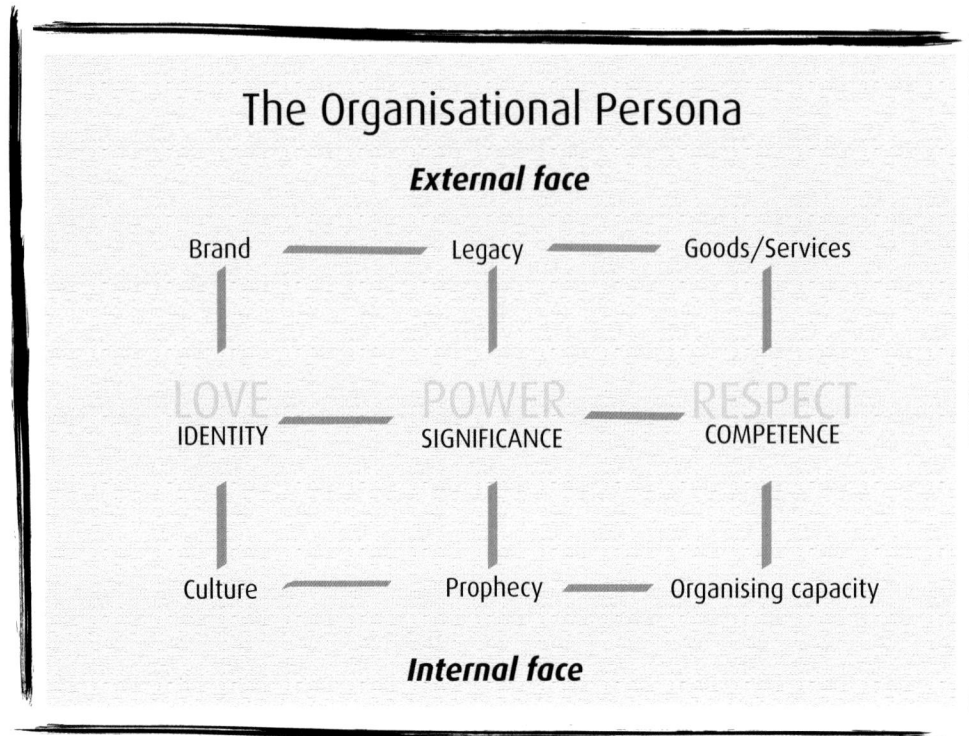

To understand this linkage and how it forms the basis of all regenerative change we need to understand what each state means – for individuals and for organisations:

Identity (Brand/Culture)

An organisation's external identity is its brand and its internal identity is its culture. Looking in, customers should be reassured to see the brand values being lived out in the way the organisation conducts itself. And looking out, employees should be proud to see their brand reflecting the way in which they work together. At its best there is a clear, transparent line of sight between the brand and the culture of an organisation.

Our recognition of what our purpose is, our needs, motivations and instincts, what we stand for and what we stand against, our values and our principles, all feed into our identity. That in turn defines the brand (the image we display to customers, consumers, and markets) and our culture. An awareness of the paradoxes that comprise our identity – the forces driving us forward (taking risks) and keeping us secure (staying safe) – is essential if we are to understand what should be retained and what discarded when rebasing and reshaping our identity. An organisation's culture/brand defines its ability to persevere with the positives of the present and be continually creative to meet the markets and its other stakeholders' future needs. Leaders need to create a transparent line of sight and palpable connection between Brand and Culture. This will create coherency and trust between the organisation and its stakeholders. Similarly, Individual leaders and teams have a need to grow and change in a differentiated way, as well as needing a sense of continuity of who they are and what they stand for.

Significance (Legacy/Prophecy)

Legacy is what we would like to create so that the organisation flourishes over time and Prophecy is what we expect to happen. The two must be married up, otherwise the organisation and its leaders will either find they are chasing unattainable futures, or failing to deliver against their capability, ending up with short-term, incremental target-setting based on the previous year's performance.

You can't predict the future, but you can invent it. You can understand the deep structure trends and patterns and engage the organisation's prophetic processes; its vision, strategy operating plans and budgets to create your version of the future.

Our significance – how powerful we want to be – is defined by our legacy and vision (what we want to happen and leave for the next generation) and our prophecy (our understanding of what may happen). Balanced prophecy is only possible once we develop an informed understanding of deep structure scenarios – the likely outcomes shaping our development. Once we can foresee probable outcomes (prophecy) we have the **practical** traction we need to move forward. This, coupled with Legacy intentions that engage and inspire, will deliver equally essential **emotional** traction. With these drivers aligned we create coherence, trust, practicality and excitement.

Individuals, to be at their best, need stretching aspirations which are rooted in what's possible. Small steps and pipe dreams can never fully satisfy the human need for accomplishment.

Competence (Services & Products/Organising Capacity)

If there is no balance between an organisation's products/services and its organising capacity, it will either be delivering sub-standard services/products to the market or failing to deliver excellent services/products for which there would be a real demand. Similarly, individuals strive for mastery of their chosen technical subject and need to communicate and influence in order to reach their goals and lead a fulfilling life. One without the other leads to frustration.

All elements of competence must work in harmony to maximise productivity.

Our competence is comprised of skills that are needed to fulfil our identity and create our legacy. These include:

- Social and functional skills.

- The capability to organise capital, property, machinery, hardware and software.

- The ability to produce relevant products and services and deliver them to the market.

- The capability to be emotionally resilient when faced with inevitable mistakes and failures.

- The skills to shape and connect all of these organising elements so that the enterprise flourishes.

Typically, organisations and individuals approach change as just a competence issue, making this the main focus of peremptory change initiatives. It is often only when an externally imposed trauma arrives that they are forced to revisit their identity and their significance. An organisation without a compelling narrative (identity and significance) must rely on its competence as its reason for existence; inevitably mistakes occur and people quickly ask, what's the point of this organisation's existence?

In fact, a crisis on one level means a crisis on all three. Rather than wait for the crisis to happen, we need to work out who we are – and what we aspire to – now. As individuals and as organisations we have to ensure that there is continuous attention and appropriate action being taken to align and interconnect our identity, significance and competence. This continual rebasing will enable individuals, teams and organisations to move toward being always relevant, always slightly ahead of their time.

From an organisational and individual point of view this means:

- Continuously and regularly spending time understanding their needs, motivations and purpose - identity.

- Using their identity as a foundation to clearly articulate and define their aspirations, the power they want to exercise in the world and what legacy they want to pass on to the next generation – significance.

- Using their understanding of who they are and what they aspire to deliver to their stakeholders to regenerate their capacity to deliver. This entails rejuvenating the framework of the organisation and themselves, their processes, procedures and channels and all the social and technical skills that enable their organisational and personal architecture to work at their best.

Building a Legacy

The significance reached through the application of our competence can be seen at three levels of accomplishment:

- **Outputs** - goals, percentage increases and decreases in single-unit measures of productivity such as turnover, headcount, production, sales.

- **Outcomes** alignments of these percentage increases and decreases into measures which could result in changes in the way stakeholders see the organisation, ROIC, share price, market share, annual profitability.

- **Legacy** changes to the fundamental nature of the way in which business is done that enable the organisation to flourish over time - the SUSTAINABLE heritage that we leave behind. The brand portfolio, technological base, market and customer relationships, competitive landscape, sustainable culture, innovative capacity, talent pool. If this is not addressed, if you don't start with the end in mind then organisations and individuals become stuck and begin to degenerate.

All three are, of course, important. But the ultimate focus – what we deliver to our stakeholders and to our successors – should be a lasting legacy.

The legacy that we pass on to the next generation - the sustainable heritage we leave behind - is what defines our significance. This deep-seated driver, in an organisational context, adds long-term value over and above the more immediate shareholder value priorities of day-to-day business.

Three Levels of Accomplishment

GENERATIONAL

Legacy
Changes to the fundamental
nature of the way in which
business is done that enables the
organisation to flourish over time -
the heritage that we leave behind

MEDIUM TERM

Outcomes
Alignments of increases and
decreases into measures which
could result in a change in the
perceived value of the organisation

SHORT TERM

Outputs
% increases and decreases in
single-unit measures such as
turnover, headcount and
production

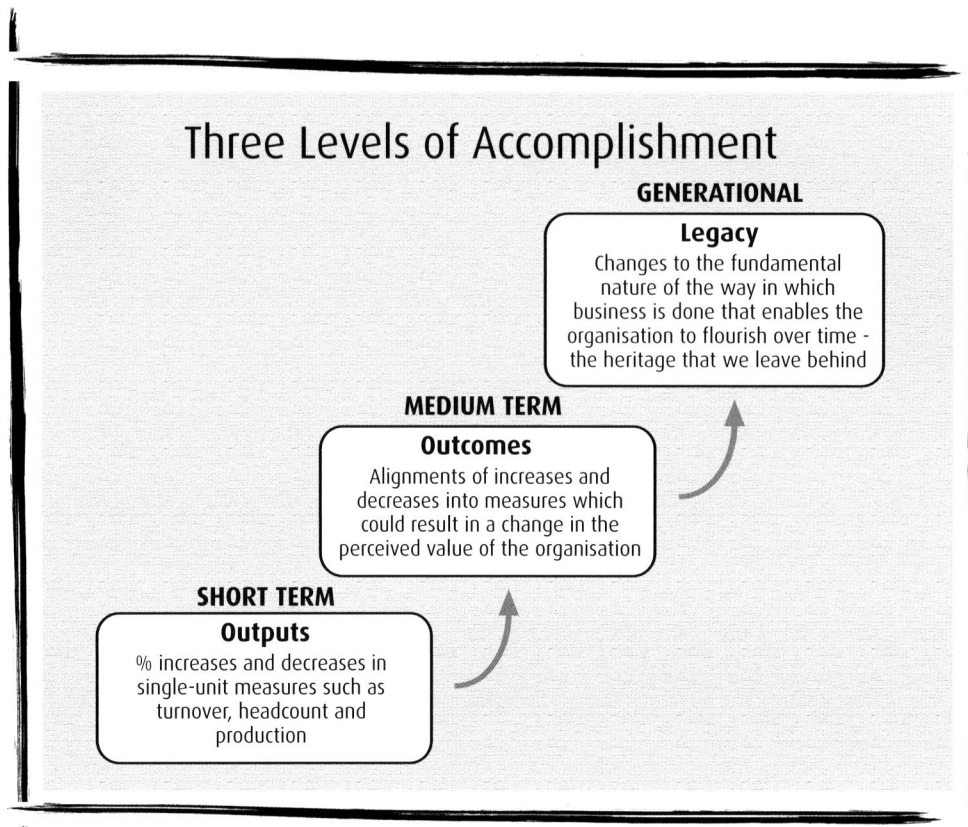

By initiating and sustaining the appropriate stakeholder conversations, business leaders become capable of fulfilling their primary function, developing a sustainable organisation by identifying patterns that help and hinder long-term accomplishment. Thus providing purpose and reason to believe and embedding regenerative change processes in the fabric of the organisation's future. This legacy-based change can take a number of forms. It may mean shifting the geographical orientation of the business from multi-local to multinational to global. It may mean shifting the position of the business in the value chain from audit to strategic evaluation, from software provider to systems integrator or from contracts draftsmen to legal risk consultants. Or it may mean changing the nature of the competitive marketplace in which the business operates, perhaps by initiating joint ventures with erstwhile competitors or by outsourcing non-core functions. It will certainly mean that everyone in the organisation needs to constantly strive to refresh, rejuvenate and regenerate their capability to suit their present and future context.

Change is not an option

The continuity of all our pasts, presents and futures can be seen in the light of need fulfilment processes. Changes are always responses to sets of unfulfilled needs – whether internally generated (desire/ambition) or externally created (economic volatility, new legislation, new technology/capability). The external reality soon becomes internalised creating particular needs that the individual or organisation must deal with. The result is action, designed to fulfil the need and resulting in new realities, new awareness and, in time, new actions.

This means that:

- We have no choice **but** to engage with change. Even doing nothing induces change activity.

- But we do have a choice about **what** and **how** we change.

- We are better equipped to make fruitful choices and changes if we **understand** the complexity and continuity of the past, present and future.

- We can re-identify ourselves so that as organisations and people we are always slightly ahead of our time, always relevant.

- We can predict-prophesy a broadband view of the future by understanding the **deep structure** of the surrounding context, the opportunities and the challenges and use this to create a legacy.

- We can regenerate our competence to fulfil our identity and reach our significance.

However, individuals and organisations tend to construct their lives to minimise the active choices they have to make. We initiate action and respond to the world in patterned ways of thinking, feeling and behaving. We strive to achieve mastery in order to maintain comfort rather than to reach for continued sustainable achievement which will always be discomforting. To disrupt this we need to initiate a pause, take the time to understand precisely where we are in the regenerative process. This will empower us to make informed choices about what we need and want and how we should think, feel and act. If, as individuals and organisations we don't take this pause for regeneration we become stuck and start to degenerate.

DEGENERATION – A NEGATIVE CHANGE CYCLE

Most individuals and therefore organisations respond to a need for change by trying to return quickly to the comfort they feel they are losing, they try to regain their equilibrium and renew their energy and effort in order to get back on track. This entails working with the surface structure of their existence, usually by trying to change the competence they bring to their existing goals, by engaging 'new' leadership or making slight changes to their behaviour in their markets and within their organisations and with their other stakeholders.

By not engaging with their past, present and future at a deep structure level, by refusing to examine their identity and significance, by insisting on being stuck in time they place themselves on the threshold of a negative change cycle, a degeneration process which becomes ever more difficult to escape from.

The three elements of degeneration are the negative shadows of the regeneration process. Identity degenerates into Anomie, love turns to disillusion and mistrust. Significance degenerates into Notoriety, power turns to entropy. Competence disintegrates into Mediocrity, respect turns to ridicule.

Anomie

Identity degenerates into Anomie when an organisation and its leaders begin to lose their sense of purpose and no longer provide clear meaning to what they and their organisation exists to do for themselves and with their stakeholders.

Organisations and leaders need to provide purpose and meaning at three levels: They are the guardians of the commercial, social, and moral compass that differentiates between the possibility of a healthy or an exploitive future for the stakeholders in the organisation.

Commercial Anomie, in organisations, sets in when there is no clear sense of the market need they exist to fulfil. Deals are therefore entered into which are punitive to self or others and the consequences of the deals effect the economic health of the organisation. It occurs when too little is paid for too much, or too much for too little. This can be a grand scale during a merger or takeover or on a seemingly small scale, getting a price point wrong by a few crucial pence.

Social Anomie is when the organisation exploits the people it employs and its other stakeholders. When the organisation treats its stakeholders as units of utility rather than human beings with legitimate needs as well as functional possibilities. Where peoples' thoughts and feelings are ignored or trampled on and where aggressive or passive behaviour is rewarded and encouraged. The obverse is also true where the emotional and physical comfort, well being and personal growth of stakeholders is seen as paramount and disconnected from the responsibility for the outcomes and legacy that the organisation is supposed to be striving for.

Moral Anomie occurs when the organisation and its leaders ignore or contradict the codes of conduct, established good practise, and the legal and ethical norms which are the foundation of its right to exist. This occurs when organisations lie to their stakeholders and use financial or physical force to exploit or benefit some stakeholders at the expense of others. When all this happens the identity of the organisation, its culture and its brand are no longer seen as trustworthy, so losing the power to retain loyalty, affection and love.

Notoriety

Significance disintegrates into Notoriety when the targeting, aiming and guiding mechanisms of leaders and their organisation begin to malfunction; they become famous for what they do badly and in the long-term become infamous. Visions and goals are either too incremental and unambitious that they fail to engage and inspire, are so arrogant and far fetched that they lead to staleness and exhaustion, or they become meaningless, repetitive mantra's where every year the budgets are set and no one believes they can be met. The ensuing cynicism about what is and what is not possible for the organisation and individuals becomes the everyday tittle tattle of the sector and the gossip of the bourse. In this way organisations and individuals lose power and become insignificant.

Mediocrity

Competence degenerates into Mediocrity when the products and services that are offered are unwanted or substandard. Mediocrity also occurs when the organising capability begins to disintegrate:

- The organisation's design does not help it meet its purpose.

- Roles and Responsibilities are unclear and contradictory.

- Technology hinders rather that enables.

- People potential is stifled rather than nurtured.

These and the hundreds of other ways in which competence can get itself into a knot can lead to a breakdown in the belief that the operational promise can be delivered which leads to even greater mediocrity ending up with a lack of self respect, and respect from stakeholders.

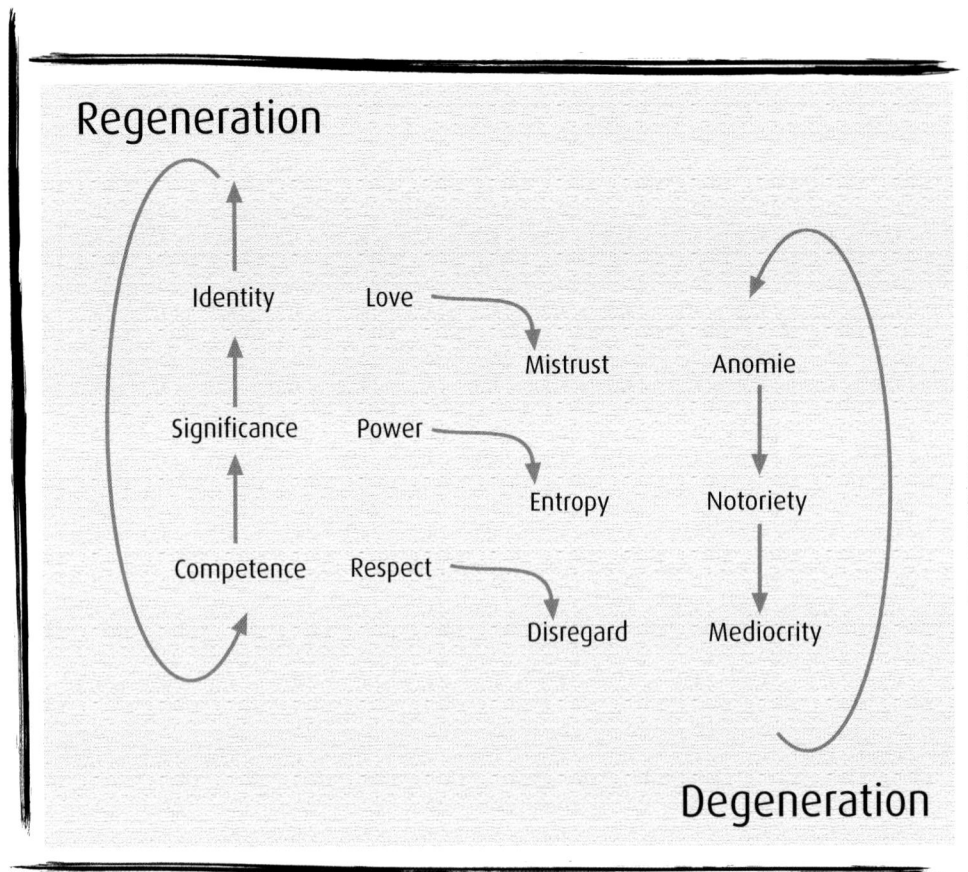

PARADOXICAL STAKEHOLDER NEEDS
The power of

All stakeholders are entwined in a relationship journey which is iterative and characterised by three phases. Joining, where foundations are laid and a footprint established. Achieving, where a mark, an imprint is made and Moving On, when a legacy is created for future generations. On entering the relationship journey it is vital to start with the end in mind so that how you join and achieve together is informed by the mutual legacy. These relationship journeys work best when they are formulated as cycles of experience with clear beginnings and endings, roles, accountabilities and relationship protocols.

There is a Hierarchy of Stakeholder Desire ranging from the brief clamour of wishes and whims, down to the tidal sweeps of need that require satisfaction over generations. These deep structure needs are usually paradoxical in nature. The different perspectives you can bring to these paradoxes range from one best way to a fully integrative view. How the need is viewed determines how it is approached, harnessed and resolved.

There are two base paradoxes for each Regenerative point which when resolved result in clear Identity, Significance and Competence.

The main distinguishing characteristics of regenerative change are therefore, its planned cyclical nature, starting from strength as well as addressing what needs to change and finding ways forward which are co-created integrative blends of the deep structure needs of all significant stakeholders.

WAVES

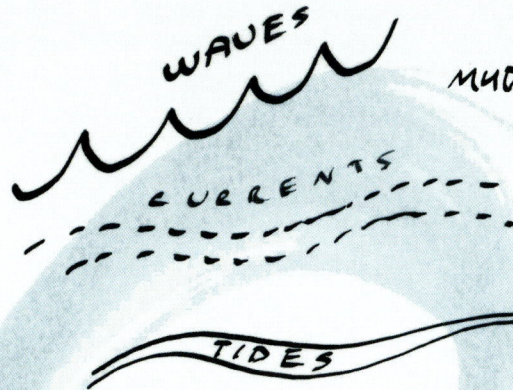

MUDDLE TO MODEL TO MUDDLE TO MODEL
IS PRECISELY WHAT
REGENERATION IS ABOUT

WHIMS
↑
WISHES
↑
WANTS
↑
NEEDS

CURRENTS

TIDES

THE VIEW YOU TAKE
DETERMINES WHAT YOU SEE
AND WHAT YOU DO

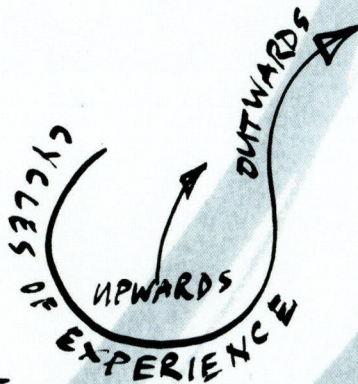

CYCLES OF EXPERIENCE
OUTWARDS
UPWARDS

PATTERNED CHANGE

CO-CREATION IS TRANSFORMATION
DONE IN RELATIONSHIP

PARADOX—
THE GRIT IN THE OYSTER
THAT SPURS INNOVATION

PARADOXICAL STAKEHOLDER NEEDS – THE POWER OF &

Choosing How to Choose

Paradox –
the Nature of Stakeholder Needs

MOVE ON

ACHIEVE

Features of
Regenerative Change

Waves, Currents
and Tides of Change

The Relationship Journey

JOIN

PARADOXICAL STAKEHOLDER NEEDS
The power of

THE RELATIONSHIP JOURNEY

Regeneration can't be done in isolation by one person trying to transform themselves or by groups trying to change other people's identity, significance and competence. It is of necessity a co-creation a transformation done is relationship.

All relationships can be characterised as journeys which can have three phases: a joining phase, an achieving phase and a moving on phase.

These are iterative and success or lack of it at any one phase determines how successful the next phase of the journey is likely to be.

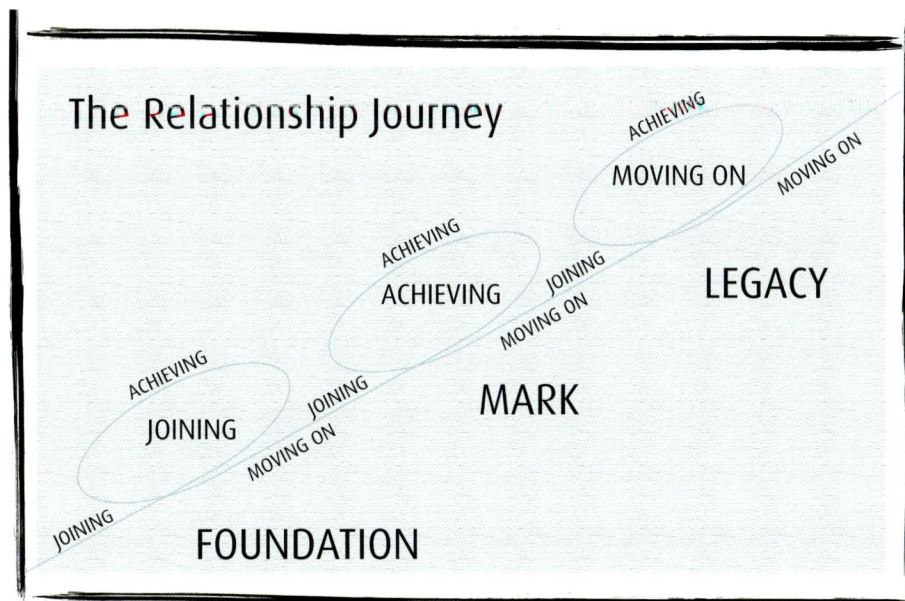

The Relationship Journey

ACHIEVING
MOVING ON
MOVING ON

ACHIEVING
ACHIEVING
JOINING
MOVING ON
LEGACY

ACHIEVING
JOINING
MARK
JOINING
MOVING ON

ACHIEVING
JOINING
MOVING ON

JOINING
FOUNDATION

A relationship means an intellectual and emotional connection which enables a joint purpose to be achieved. So, relationships are not just between people, but also between people and property, people and technology, people and artefacts, people and ideas.

Joining

So Joining can be about:

- Joining a new organisation.

- A merger or acquisition.

- A new way of thinking and/or doing.

- Engaging with another individual, team or group.

- Moving house/office.

- Buying the latest PC or mobile phone.

- Starting a new job.

- Getting married.

- Acquiring a new car.

Anywhere a new connection is made where both parties, animate, semi-animate or inanimate need to interact to achieve a purpose over time.

In the regeneration process, joining is the phase where foundations can be laid, architecture can be drawn, process and protocol can be agreed, principles and future vision can be established and joint purpose can be forged.

The ability to connect to depth quickly, to join fully, to commit intellectually and emotionally to common purpose has a profound effect on how successful and fulfilling a relationship can be. To accept a new job because it's expected of you, to buy a software package because it's the latest fad, to buy a company at an inflated price as a consequence of an ego fuelled need to win, to walk down the aisle knowing you are making a mistake ensure that it's very difficult to achieve what the original intention or need was. This is particularly debilitating and dispiriting if, because of lack of seeming alternatives or courage, the relationship is allowed to continue for longer than it serves its purpose.

Regeneration needs the oxygen of new relationships. New doesn't just mean completely different. It is possible to work for the same organisation, to have the same job title, to work in the same office, live in the same house, be married or living with the same partner for long periods of time and still feel that you are at the beginning of your next great adventure. This is usually because the nature of the relationship has been changed to suit the context the relationship exists in. Even in what can be called long lasting, stable relationships it is likely there will have been a number of regenerative points where rejoining, reconnecting in a different way has occurred. Indeed it is likely that these rejoining, regenerating points are instrumental in making the relationship stable and long lasting.

Making sure the joining phase of the relationship is as productive as it can be also means that you have to have a clear idea of what you want to accomplish in the achieving phase and a current view of the legacy you want to leave when moving on. Preparing for the full cycle of the relationship journey, starting with the end in mind is just as important as the immersion in the early stages of joining. Also, the pattern is embedded in itself so that every Joining phase has an achieving and moving on phase, every achieving phase has a joining and moving on phase and every moving on phase has a joining and achieving phase. All three are always present; one will be more prominent in the foreground with the other two working steadily away in the background. So birth, a predominantly joining phase, has a phase of achievement and moving on. Adulthood with achieving in the foreground has joining and moving on in the background and old age though predominantly a moving on phase has many joining and achieving facets.

There will be a relationship journey with each of our stakeholders. Organisations and individuals will sometimes believe that they can be independent of at least some of their stakeholder's needs. The reality is that if another party has a vested interest in an organisation or individual's success or failure then they are in a relationship and that relationship needs to be managed, even ignoring a constituency defines the nature of the ongoing relationship.

Finding and forging common purpose with stakeholders and building robust relationships, early on, which will withstand the inevitable difficulties that all relationships encounter is the hall mark of a successful joining phase. Joining has to be a joint endeavour and this ensures there will be many magical moments of connected enlightenment when stakeholders notice that their joint overarching ambition can transcend many of their real differences. However, one party often has to initiate what can be a difficult iterative process that needs perseverance, toughness and generosity before common purpose can be forged and joining achieved.

Joining is often seen as an inconvenience to be ignored or rushed through rather than the wonderful opportunity to get the basics right, taking time to pause to prophesy, to rebase not just adjust, to regenerate yourself and your relationships in the light of your accumulated learning. This attention to the joining phase really pays off in the achieving and moving on phase. There is often a drive for immediate chemistry and an expectation that this immediate full contact should always happen. People are often left to flounder with no useful induction when joining a company other than some cursory introductions, to make sense of a dense jargon rich manual on how their new I.T. product should operate or to deal with the practical consequences of a 'dream' takeover where the lack of complementariness of market or offering was overlooked by hastily done, ill conceived due diligence.

The capability to join usefully is dependant also, on how cleanly closure was completed in the previous moving on phase. Does the fact that we miss the functionality of our old mobile phone, still pine over our first true love, are still convinced that our previous strategy was the right one, still believe against all evidence that life under the previous regime was better for everybody stop us from usefully joining the next phase of our relationship journeys. Giving attention to what we are letting go and how to manage the cusp between moving on and joining deserves discussion so that we don't burn the library and take forward the best of what was into joining, with the potential of a new future.

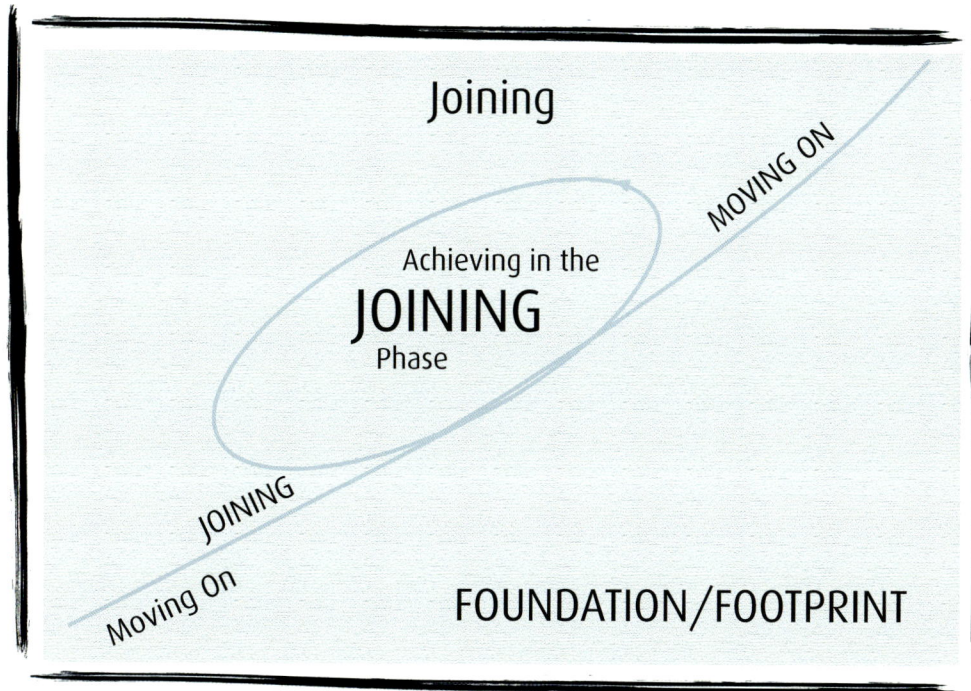

Joining

MOVING ON

Achieving in the
JOINING
Phase

JOINING

Moving On

FOUNDATION/FOOTPRINT

Achieving

If joining is about clearing the ground, building a foundation and creating the architecture for a new Identity, Significance and Competence, then achieving is about building on this foundation by transforming and embodying the new Identity, driving toward the goals of how Significant we want to be by expressing our Competence at its highest level. It's about:

- Mobilising and aligning energy.

- Creating traction between inputs and outputs.

- Reaching objectives and targets.

- Performing in all areas of endeavour.

- Fulfilling real stakeholder needs rather than ephemeral whims and wishes.

- Making a real difference.

- Making a mark.

If the joining phase of the relationship journey with the stakeholder groups has led to agreed common purpose, then the power of both ends of the relationship can be harnessed, so that shareholders are working to make the executive succeed and vice versa, the organisation and its suppliers are both maximising effort toward a common future and leaders and followers are joining in a sustaining dance that will pay off for all parties.

It is in the achieving phase that abiding trust can be created. Trust is an output as well as an input to relationships. No matter how sparkly clean the joining phase has been there will be inevitable confusions, difficulties, mistakes and breakdowns in relationship. How these are dealt with determines the amount and nature of trust that evolves. The day to day operations of a relationship mean that compromise will occur, goals will become diluted and custom and practise will become entrenched in more or less useful patterns. To minimise the risk of not reaching common purpose, relationships need transparent feedback loops that see break downs as opportunities, not just to recover the relationship, but to take it to new heights of effectiveness. Therefore there will be a need for many mini iterations of joining, achieving and moving on as part of the overall achieving phase.

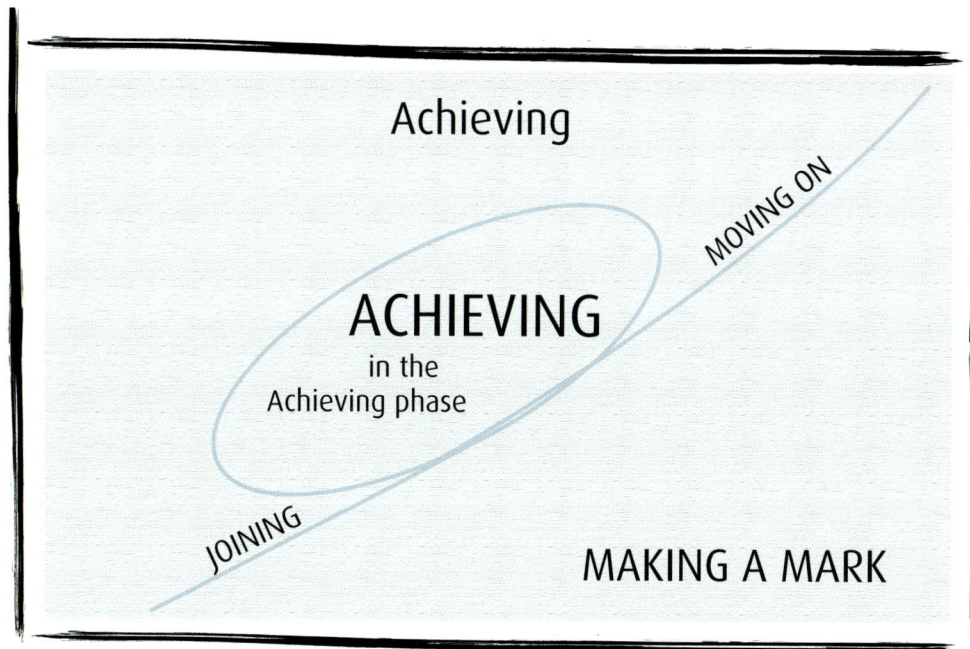

Achieving

MOVING ON

ACHIEVING
in the
Achieving phase

JOINING

MAKING A MARK

Moving On

Planning to move on, to leave, to stop, is often a discomforting, no-go area of human endeavour. Even seemingly positive futures such as retirement, promotion or marriage produce disequilibrium and therefore stress. It is in most of our natures to create and/or seek out a comfortable existence and to stay with it no matter how uncomfortable that comfort becomes, we strive not so that we can strive again more potently next time. We mainly strive to overcome challenges and realise opportunities, to reach a stable state. We try to protect and prolong what we have created/won/achieved rather than see the achievement as the cue to move on and regenerate, to focus on what we need to do next. The need to move on can be and is ignored even when all the alarm bells are signalling an acute need for change. Comfort doesn't necessarily mean pleasure, its more what we are used to. Even the most extreme wake up calls are treated as snooze alarms allowing short-term, ameliorative response to the immediate signal, rather than a call to fundamentally regenerate how we meet our present and future needs.

Moving on is sometimes associated with failure, probably because it is seldom planned for. We are often only aware of the need to move on after we have overstepped the point when we were performing at our peak in our present context, or we were repeating ever more sterile patterns of thinking and behaving to reach our comfortable goals, rather than regenerating ourselves to the next phase.

Fundamentally:

- It's hard to find a purpose for existence once, let alone keep refreshing or regenerating it.

- It's hard to engage and inspire ourselves and others to pursue a joint ambition, let alone keep finding more and different people to do it with.

- We don't want to die, let alone kill part of what we have achieved on purpose, so that we can start more productively again in the service of a higher plane of fulfilment.

The inevitability of being present at and scared of the many moving on points we all experience in our lives, as well as coming to terms with our final death, makes it less likely that we will plan to move on even though the best time to start with the end in mind would be at the beginnings of our many journeys.

Cycles of Experience

Where clear cycles of experience are mapped out, when clear protocols about moving on are agreed and transparent then moving on to do the next important piece of work will be equated with building the next future rather than punishment for past achievement.

Cycles of experience work when there is clarity about the duration and nature of the cycle. This can be a strategic time frame, a term of office, the nature of a joint venture, the legal life of a contract. The cycle has a predetermined end which means those involved will know when time is up on this particular piece of their journey.

Cycles of experience, Joining, Achieving, Moving On, need to be of a substantial length. In our complex and ambiguous world, it is not likely that a useful full cycle will take less than two years and in our constantly changing context, taking more than four to five years before engaging with regeneration becomes dangerous.

The ways in which we bring about closure in order to move on need to be addressed in a more innovative manner. Our world is constructed in both an hierarchical and an organic interlinked way. We recognise our success and fulfilment by both progression through a hierarchy and our more organic capability to master new forms of endeavour. It is possible to gain status, to be differentiated, both through our position and through mastery. Organisations and individuals still generally see reward as hierarchical, only some people can succeed and therefore move on to the next echelon. However, it is possible to view cycles of experience which not only lead up the hierarchy, but to new associated areas of mastery. It is something of a shock for Presidents to notice that they can have a more fulfilling, global statesman role after their statutory term as President ends; for CEOs to find they can work more usefully with the fabric of capitalism in private equity rather than at the head of a single organisation no matter how significant; for a successful investor to use their wealth not to just accumulate more, but to effect a change in some of the world's more intractable problems. It is possible to enable people to move on in ways which ensure dignity from cradle to grave.

Being clear about what the cycles of experience are and can be for each stakeholder grouping enables moving on to be both upwards and outwards. Knowing that moving on is clearly inevitable fosters innovation in the moving on process.

Moving on needs to be measured by and signalled as the leaving of a legacy, a bequest, the generation of an ongoing heritage. Then the presence of the organisation and the person and the power of the relationships can live over generations and the spirit and the consequences of their action remain when the particular people move on.

Planning to, and delivering a legacy; the fundamental changes in the stakeholder relationships that enrich ongoing generations is the focus of the moving on phase. Moving on can create new energy rather than a vacuum and create healthy possibilities for productive joining in the next generation of the journey. The cusp between moving on and new joining is best marked by completion and celebration. Instituting rites of passage where what has been left unsaid is spoken with generosity, achievements are feasted upon, heartfelt thank yous are given and received, forgiveness is granted and goodbyes and au revoirs are elegantly exchanged will ensure that all parties join their next relationship journey with energy and a positive spirit.

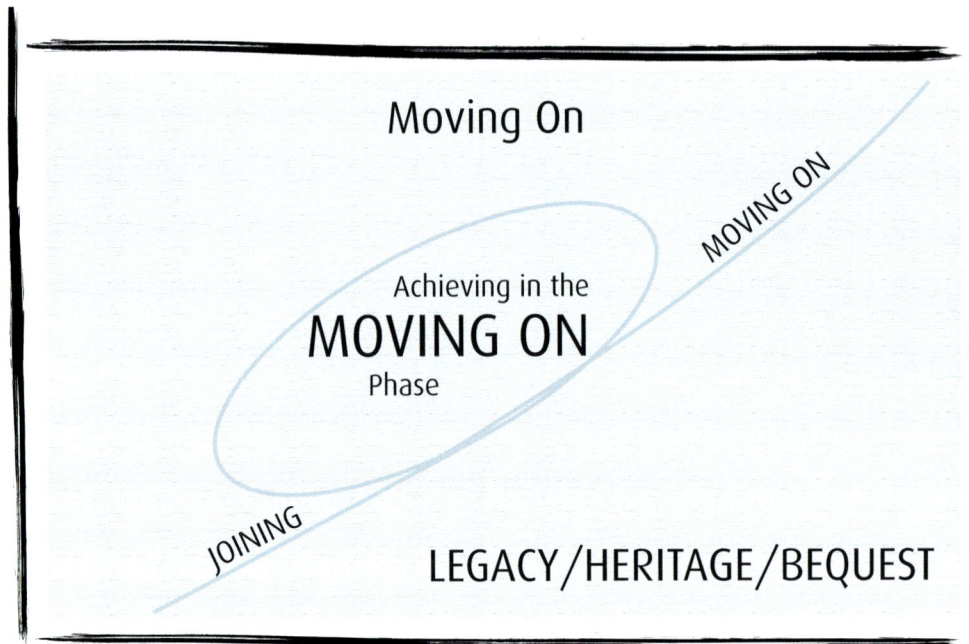

Moving On

Achieving in the
MOVING ON
Phase

MOVING ON

JOINING

LEGACY/HERITAGE/BEQUEST

Relationships, organisations and the people in them are always therefore on the threshold of profound periods of change. There is always a star to reach, a mountain to climb, a chasm to fall into and another emerging need to satisfy. When these always present opportunities, needs, are noticed, people mobilise themselves to satisfy the need. They also, however, mobilise themselves to resist change. These are thresholds, moments of felt opportunity and resistance and the resistance generated by the opportunity can become non rational negativity and cynicism, adversely affecting attempts at regeneration and holding back the fruitful satisfaction of the stakeholder need.

The challenge is to view change thresholds as opportunities for personal, professional and profitable regeneration and resistance as a natural part of the relationship journey and a legitimate focus for the regenerative process.

The regenerative and relationship journey insists that we are aware of a deep structure to how things were and how they can be. From an everyday perspective this 'order' or 'nature' appears unending and unyielding. But needs do change. When they do, it is because of a blend of subtle accumulated changes of evolution and dramatic revolutionary changes. However, even apparently revolutionary changes evolve over time and can be predicted and managed. As the nature/nurture debate unfolds we are becoming more aware that everything was once space dust and of how deeply we are a product of our genetic inheritance and also how even that basic hardwiring does change. No matter how programmed we are, the one point of choice we will always have is the perspective we bring to the context we are in and therefore the nuance of action we take. Deep, structure changes form part of a recognisable, long-term flow – a tidal pattern. Understanding the structure allows for regeneration that is capable of aligning immediate actions with long-term patterns. Tidal flows, properly harnessed, deliver great power.

WAVES, CURRENTS AND TIDES OF CHANGE

Deep structure needs influence and control surface developments. Take as an analogy the world's tidal flows – great global sweeps of movement interacting with more localised currents, which, in turn, control the waves which shape the contours of coastlines.

Most change attempts only affect the short-term wave patterns. As a result, only mediocre adjustments are made. Not enough attempt is made to notice – let alone harness – the power of the stakeholder needs embodied in the socio-technical/commercial/political tides which actually determine the movement of currents and waves across the globe.

By understanding how they work and what influence they have, regeneration can be planned which is in tune with unfolding long-term processes. This is what prophesy is all about – **understanding the tidal rhythms of change.**

Waves – Currents – Tides

Waves – Time-bound regeneration projects
Currents – Influences that affect the waves
Tides – Deep structure patterns of changes in need unfolding in our markets and society

Waves

Change Agendas

The ideal is to get all the waves breaking on the beach at the right time, in sequence. This can only be done by understanding the deep structures, the primary needs of our stakeholders. This understanding, this commitment to prophesy is the bedrock. Without it a sense of vision and legacy (a coherent strategy) is unattainable.

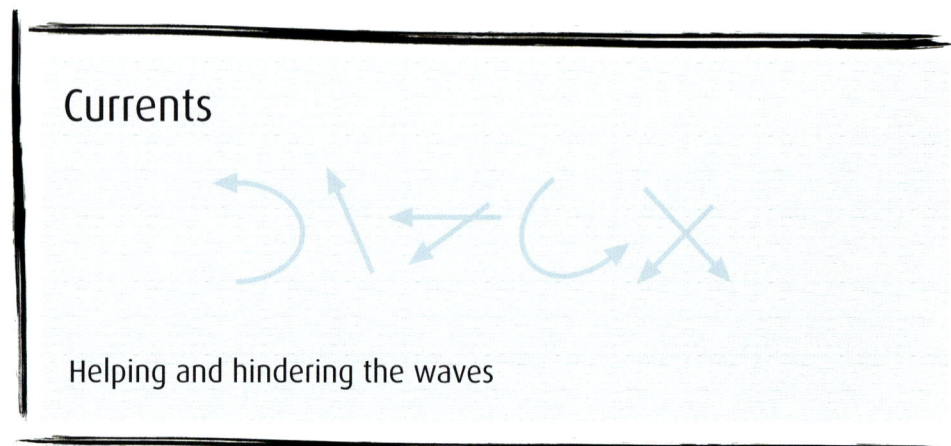

Currents

Helping and hindering the waves

Tides

Deep structure patterns of need

Being able to co-create a prophecy with stakeholders at a tide and current level, to have a sense of the complexity of the past/present and use this to formulate a broadband view of what the future holds for all parties allows us to make more useful predictions at the wave level (if we steer this way, in these conditions, then the consequences/destination will be .....). In other words, we can't predictably steer a boat if we can't prophesy what the tides and currents of that area will do.

By acquiring an understanding of the joint, deep structure, instead of skimming the surfaces of our stakeholder relationships, we move from building our future on the coarse templates of the past to being able to co-design new modes and ways of regenerating for all significant parties.

Whims/ Wishes/ Wants/ Needs

This is a hierarchy of desire where whims are short lived, quickly moving spikes of appetite, wishes are wistful hopes for a better future, wants are the clamorous often contradictory calls to medium-term action and needs are deep patterns of urge that demand satisfaction to enable long term sustainability.

Most organisations are awash with managers' or customers' whims and wishes and what the analysts and owners wants is often loud and clear, however, less attention is given to the deeper abiding needs of an organisation and all its significant stakeholders.

This is probably because the real needs have been buried under years of established practise, this is what was always done and this is the way we've always done it. Also, what stakeholders want is often in the moment in direct contradiction with what they would, over a longer term, need.

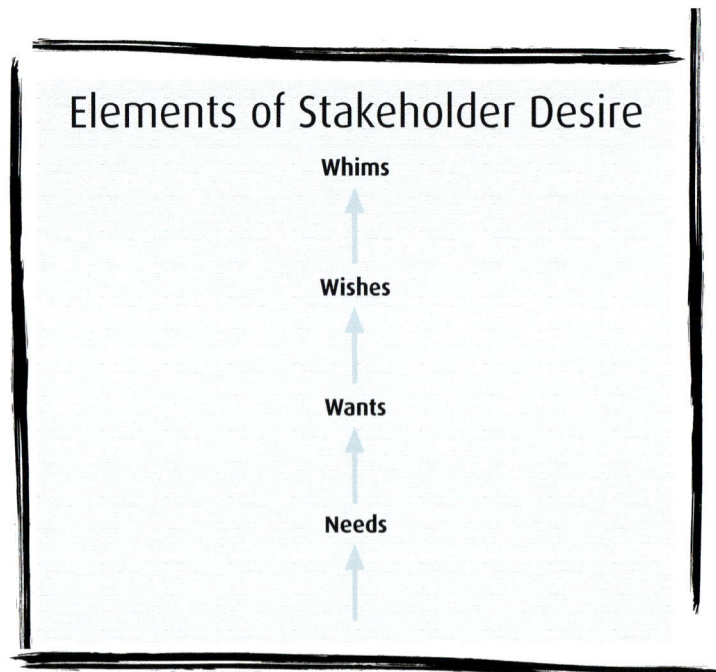

Elements of Stakeholder Desire

Whims

↑

Wishes

↑

Wants

↑

Needs

↑

These should inform each other but there is often distortion and disconnect between needs and whims. Stakeholder needs are also hard to pin down, in that at a fundamental level they are paradoxical and can be viewed as contradictory. So, a seemingly simple need for profit will contain the paradoxical need for healthy present earnings whilst investing for future growth. There needs to be a virtuous cycle between the two for profit to continually happen. A need for the lowest possible price seems clear for a purchaser until they realise it should not be at the expense of the other need which is for a continuous sustainable supply. The need for jobs can only be usefully seen in conjunction with the need for work to create added value, this virtuous cycle needs to happen for anybody to have a job. Which piece of the paradox is weight given to, which need supplants which? These questions lead to dilemmas where you seem to need to sacrifice, at least in the short term, the satisfaction of a perfectly legitimate need to support another connected one.

Thankfully, paradox does not always lead to dilemma and the painful choices that go with being between a rock and a hard place, or heaven and nirvana. You can get the best of both, you can have your cake and eat it.

Harnessing the best of both

THE POWER OF
Choosing how to choose

If you are in the habit of seeing dilemmas, you will see them. However, once the seemingly paradoxical needs are clear, it is possible to find integrative, best of both world approaches and outcomes. There is always a choice as to how you view options and the mindset you choose to see challenges and opportunities will determine the action you engage in to meet the need.

How organisations and individuals view the past, present and future will determine the choices they make about what and how they change to meet their own and their stakeholder needs.

When they notice a clear strong strand of what has made them and their organisation successful they are likely to make choices about their future based on that formula for success, copying, building and perhaps amplifying on this one best way of constructing the future.

If the dilemmas of their pasts and the hard choices of their present are foremost in their minds they are likely to construct their future options as a set of either/or choices, choosing one path which precludes them from another.

If their view of their past success is that it is due to a series of judicious compromises then their mode of prophecy will be a balanced one where extreme choices are smoothed to a point where small degrees of seemingly opposing choices can be done at the same time.

If they have a sense that they have steered a path toward success and away from failure by sequencing changes appropriately, getting the best from one course of action before reversing course and doing the opposite for a while. Then they are likely to look forward in a pendulum swing mindset where they sequence choices for action rather than do them in parallel.

These are all useful mindsets and in a specific context will all be the 'right' approach to take to regeneration at a particular point in time. Individuals and organisations, however, are not always aware of the patterns of choice they bring to the point of transformation, not noticing that the manner in which they view the world can condemn them to make the same blinkered mistakes as in their past or not capture and utilise the innovation and creativity available at the present threshold of change.

There are two other ways of thinking and feeling when addressing regeneration.

Firstly to prophesy and plan action to happen in tandem not in sequence, for seemingly contradictory actions to run in parallel each informing the other as to what adjustments need to take place to maximise the satisfaction of all needs that are in play.

Finally, most contradictions can be viewed with an integrative mindset. How do we get the best out of both poles of the dilemma? What's the innovative creative spark that changes the rules of the game or the game itself so that the paradox is satisfied? For example, to share industry best practise with our competitors and for different service providers to share a common technological platform.

Therefore there are six mind/feeling sets with which we can approach attempts to meet stakeholder needs:

- The one best way mindset.
- The either/or mindset.
- The balanced mindset.
- The pendulum swing mindset.
- The parallel mindset.
- The both/and mindset.

One Best Way – Change is initiated from the thought and feeling base that dictates that there is only one way forward from a burning platform or toward an ideal future. This approach can lead to forceful action for difference and at best leads to real commitment and traction. At its worst it ignores all other possible choices and can result in lurching from one negative reality to the next or chasing unattainable dreams.

Either/Or – Change here is initiated by the mind/felling set that dictates that all choice is polarised. You have two choices and choosing one means you can not have the power of the other choice. At its best this gives focus and moves you to the upside of one best way, at its worst it leads to "unhappy remembering" of what might have happened if you'd chosen the other alternative and "trepidatious looking forward" to the awful future we are bound to face as a consequence of our poor choice.

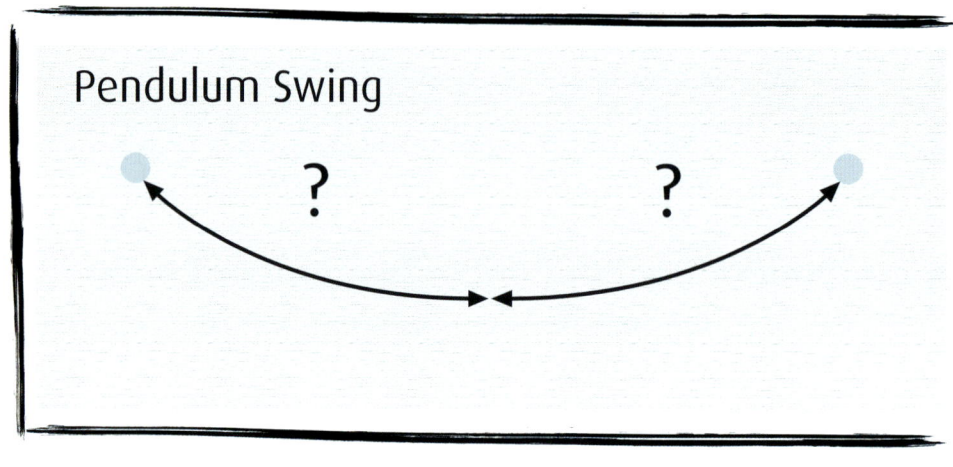

Pendulum Swing – This mind/feeling set provides reassurance that even when faced with two options we can get the best of both by doing one now and the other later. The positive of this is that you are getting the best of both options but at different times. The down side is that it is seen to be contradictory to those engaged within the change and also doesn't get the best of both choices at the same time.

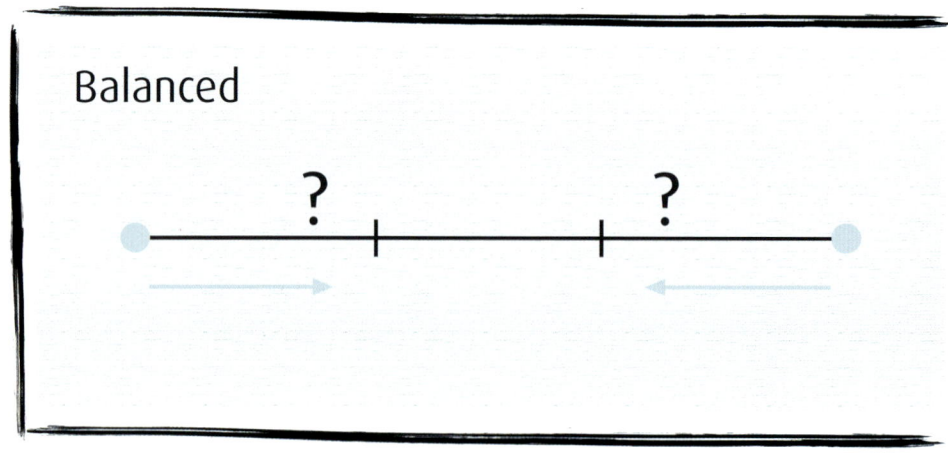

Balanced – This approach solves the dilemma of seemingly contradictory choices by diluting the poles of possibility so you end up doing a bit of both. A balanced approach at its best gives you some of each option.

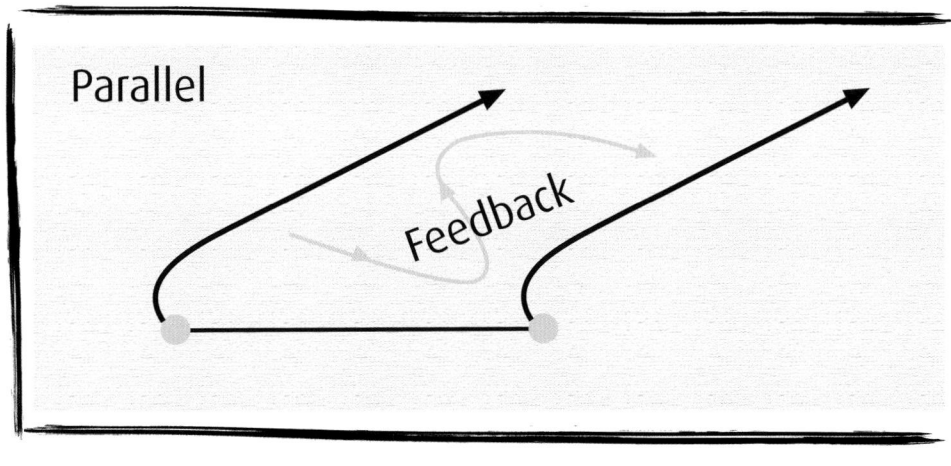

Parallel – This mindset takes all the strands of the paradox along together connected by feedback loops so as to maximise the satisfaction of both legitimate needs. Growing and shrinking, weeding and seeding, high tech, high touch.

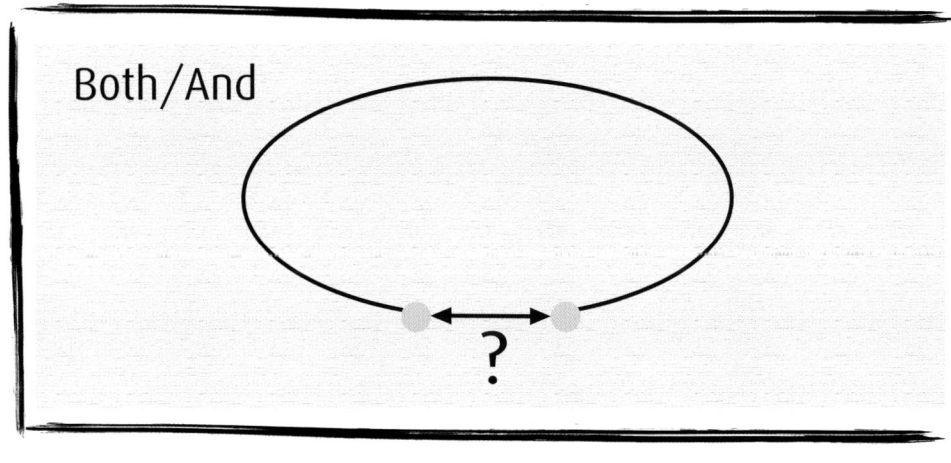

The Both/And – This approach reframes choices as opportunities for integrating activity in creative ways which harness the best of both of the options. This best of both approach is at the heart of regenerative change.

Once it is possible to identify the paradoxical stakeholder needs that are in play and bring the right mindsets to them we are closer to understanding the patterns that underlie regenerative change.

Harnessing paradoxes

People and organisations are driven by complex combinations of paradoxes. For example, there is a basic need for growth – encapsulating both a need to change and a need to remain the same. To change what isn't useful and keep and finely tune what is.

On an organisational level these paradoxes might include:

- The distilling industry, which needs to protect and sell its heritage, while engaging seriously with new product development.

- Retailers needing generalist out of town superstores and tightly-focused town and city shops.

- An energy company reinventing itself as a sustainable business.

- A clothing retailer combining low cost manufacturing processes whilst inviting intense NGO scrutiny of its ethical procurement policy.

- A fast-food business regenerating itself as a provider of fast-food and healthy meals.

- The automotive industry searching for an efficient petrol engine and striving for acceptable and efficient electrical cars.

- International organisations that need to be global and multi-local.

- Any organisation which to prosper must efficiently combine centralised and decentralised decision-making processes.

If ignored, these paradoxes can be destructive – breeding discord, aimlessness and indecision. But properly recognised and integrated they provide stimuli for action and success. In healthy organisations paradoxes are the irritants that spark growth – the grit in the oyster that spurs innovation. Instead of swinging from extreme to extreme, or failing to embrace either, organisations can and should combine the apparently contradictory – becoming traditional and creative, large and small, profitable and sustainable.

All organisations are playing out these paradoxes – some unconsciously, unwillingly, destructively, others consciously and productively.

Paradoxes enable us to see the whole picture – and where we fit into it.

All our **Needs** are inherently paradoxical – open to actions which:

- Ensure the satisfaction of the need so that attention can be given to new, emerging needs and a positive regenerative cycle is evoked.

- Allow the need to become an intermittent irritant where similar dilemmas crop up because the underlying issues are not dealt with.

- Ensure the need becomes a life-long struggle as the needs are not met, producing degenerative negative cycles.

Understood – and harnessed – paradoxes become engines for growth, barometers of change and signposts to the future. Because there is always a need for regeneration and as most change requires human intervention or participation, key paradoxes will run through any organisation.

The Paradoxes of Identity, Significance, and Competence
The Need for Identity (who we are)

The paradoxes that lie at the heart of an organisation's identity are the need to remain the same and the need to change and the need to be individual and the need to be similar. Stimulated by the necessity for growth and differentiation, these seemingly contradictory needs can be resolved into powerful drivers for the brand, its external identity and the culture, its internal identity. As the fuel of the organisation the identity must be constantly revitalised and refreshed in the light of current surrounding circumstances. This calls for ongoing self-examination by the organisations and its leaders of their needs, instincts, values and beliefs, what they stand for and against, their deep motivations and their ongoing purpose within the organisation and with their external stakeholders.

The need to change and the need to remain the same must operate in a virtuous cycle.

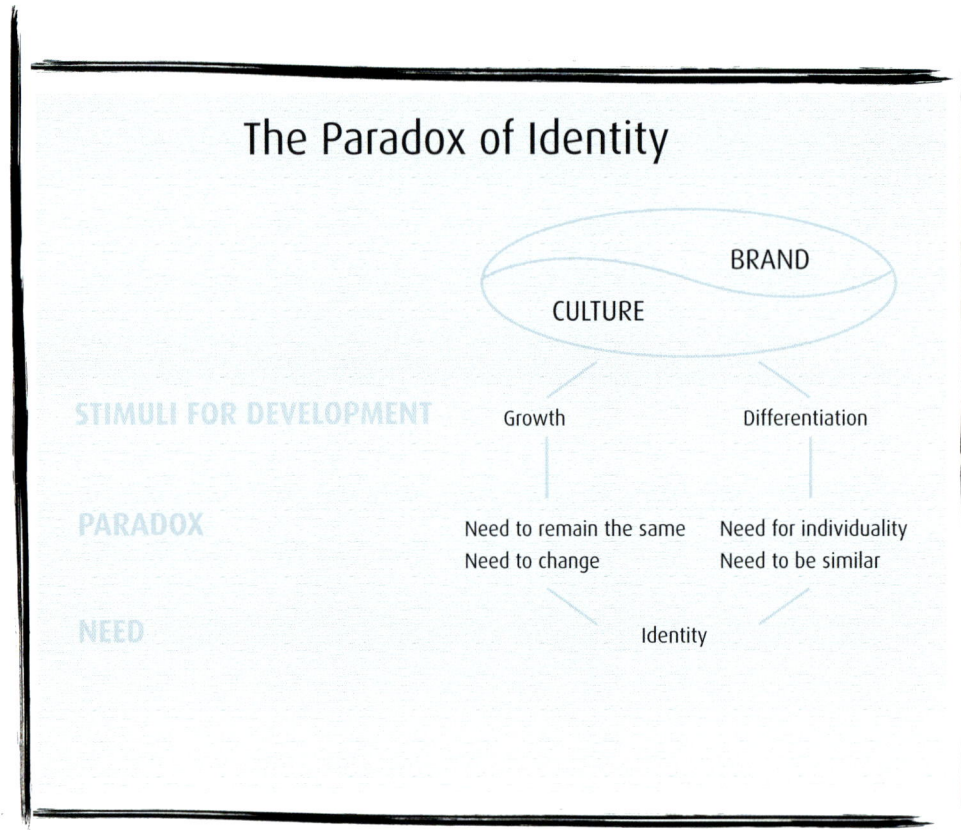

The Paradox of Identity

	CULTURE / BRAND	
STIMULI FOR DEVELOPMENT	Growth	Differentiation
PARADOX	Need to remain the same Need to change	Need for individuality Need to be similar
NEED		Identity

Examples of transforming what needs to change and amplifying or tuning what needs to be retained could be an established luxury brand regenerating itself to provide bikinis and contemporary fashions alongside a modern reworking of its traditional product range; a multinational law firm retaining its status as a local trusted business adviser to core corporate clients in its home market, while developing and expanding its operations and capabilities on a global scale; or a supermarket chain can upgrade to prestige goods and services whilst building its reputation for low cost.

Just how organisations resolve this paradox will dictate how effectively they deal with growth. This process will determine their culture – and their brand essence. If no useful resolution is met then the organisation and individuals will drift toward Anomie with no star to steer toward, no compass and no trust in relationships.

The other connected paradox underpinning the identity of organisations and the individuals who comprise them is the need to be individual and the need to be similar.

This is the paradoxical need to be a powerfully distinctive member of an affinity group. To stand out and to be part of. Examples would be a cosmetics manufacturer selling similar new products to its competitors while illuminating itself via advertising; or a software provider needing to create products that dovetail with existing applications while distinguishing itself and boosting its revenues by the nature of the support services it provides. Similarly, a bank needs the ability to be seen as discreet by its core high net worth clients, whilst positioning itself as primus interpares with its high volume retail competitors, a tax adviser needs the ability to provide clients with creative financial planning while ensuring that it remains well within all relevant regulatory and legal frameworks.

This kind of resolution leads to differentiation for individuals, organisations and stakeholders.

In summary the need for identity is underpinned by the two sets of paradox and how these are resolved will lead to particular expressions of growth and differentiation which will determine the brand and the culture.

How this is resolved will define how stakeholders view the organisation and what kind of emotional bond they can forge with it. This gives a motif of what the organisation needs to look and feel like in order to regenerate sustainable growth.

The elements of identity need to work together consistently and transparently so that stakeholders all perceive the added value generated by the virtuous cycle of culture and brand working together. If this is done, the purpose, the reason an organisation exists or the persona individuals want to fulfil will be clear to all stakeholders

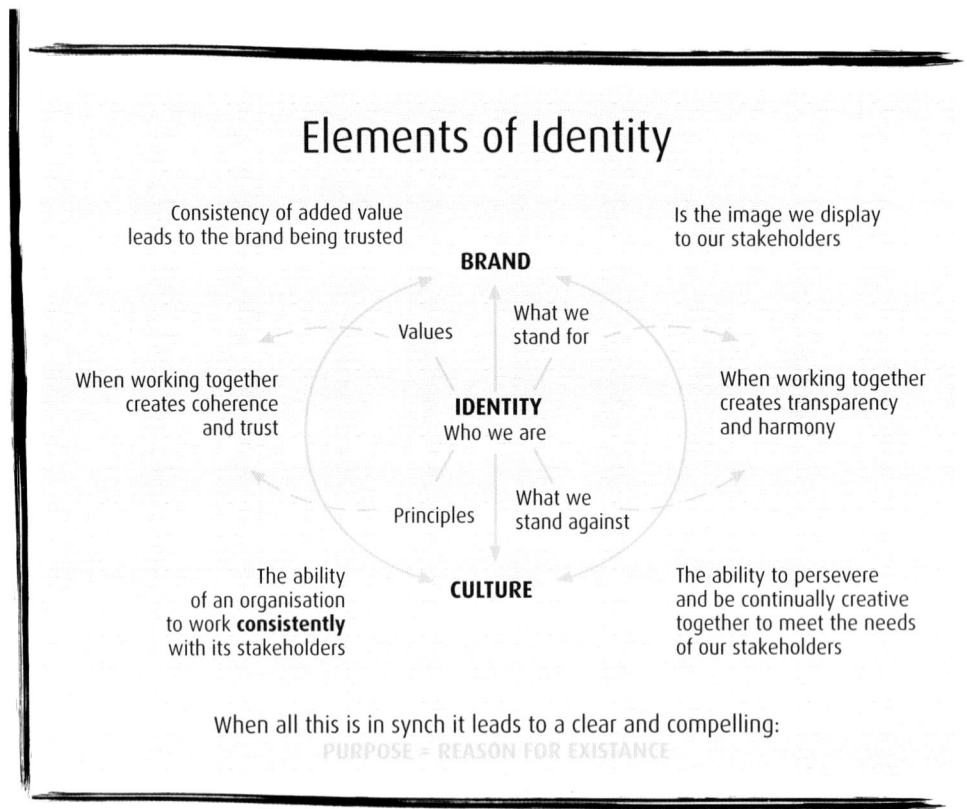

Elements of Identity

Consistency of added value
leads to the brand being trusted

Is the image we display
to our stakeholders

BRAND

Values | What we stand for

When working together
creates coherence
and trust

When working together
creates transparency
and harmony

IDENTITY
Who we are

Principles | What we stand against

The ability
of an organisation
to work **consistently**
with its stakeholders

CULTURE

The ability to persevere
and be continually creative
together to meet the needs
of our stakeholders

When all this is in synch it leads to a clear and compelling:
PURPOSE = REASON FOR EXISTANCE

The Need for Significance - how powerful we want to be

The elements stemming from a need for significance which, when effectively combined, provide organisations and individuals with the gravitational pull that keeps them moving forward are legacy and prophecy. The legacy vision, what they would like to happen, combined with the prophecy, what they expect to happen must be married up and in synch. Otherwise, in an organisational context, the leadership will find itself either chasing unattainable futures or failing to deliver its promises. The stimuli drawing the resolution of these paradoxes is the necessity to always improve productivity, coupled with the need for ambitions to be constantly fulfilled.

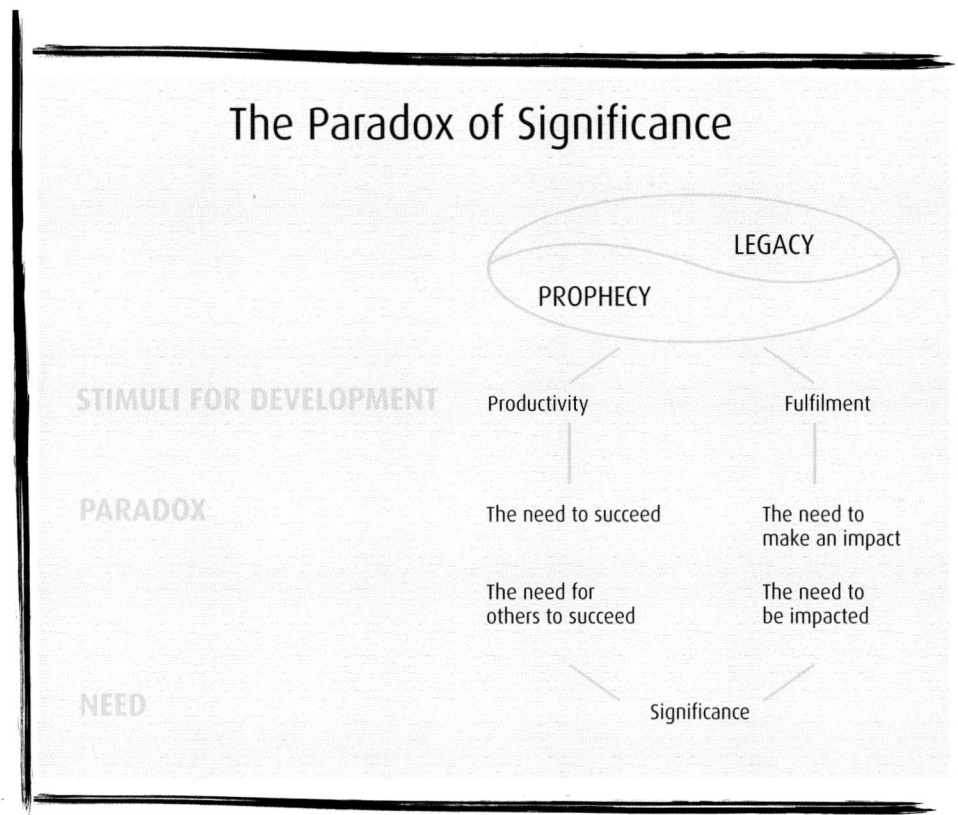

The Paradox of Significance

	LEGACY	
	PROPHECY	

STIMULI FOR DEVELOPMENT	Productivity	Fulfilment
PARADOX	The need to succeed	The need to make an impact
	The need for others to succeed	The need to be impacted
NEED		Significance

Twin paradoxes lie at the heart of the need for significance. The need for success for self and others and the need for all stakeholders to make a maximum impact, for the real power of the organisation to make a difference so that everyone feels fulfilled, not just successful.

- The need to succeed.

- The need for others to succeed.

In our interdependent world, to succeed, to be productive, we need others to bring their success, their productivity to us. Our goals and measures are interlocked so that unless everyone succeeds in their part of the value chain productivity will be sub-optimal. Useful prophecy is only possible when everyone tries to foster each others' success.

Examples would be the need for an organisation's suppliers to be making a fair profit while the organisation satisfies its shareholders' demands; the need for joint venture organisations to pursue their individual goals without upsetting the balance of the collaborative relationship in which they are involved; or the preparedness of a knowledge-creating business to license out its intellectual property to potential competitors, while securing financial benefits from this relinquishing of control.

Their resolution leads to productivity which, in turn, feeds into Legacy and Prophesy. At the same time there is the need to resolve:

- The need to make an impact.

- The need to be impacted.

All individuals and organisations want to make a lasting impact - not just succeed at meeting their immediate goals - both are necessary for real fulfilment. To do this they will have to harness the power of others to make a lasting difference, not just reach the next goal. Enabling all stakeholders to make a lasting impact on each other will build a virtuous cycle where the combined impact will fundamentally change not just how things are done but what needs to be done. The intrinsic feelings of fulfilment that stem from this push the bounds of what is believed to be possible so that a lasting legacy can be formed and delivered.

Prophecy and Legacy vision together create intellectual and emotional traction for moving forward, combining inspirational leadership with comfort-giving experience and insight. In an organisational context, when these two forces are working together, the overall benefit will be coherence, trust, excitement and propulsion.

Elements of Significance

A wise guide based on deep knowledge, learning and insight

Provokes intellectual and practical traction for moving forward

Prophecy
What will probably happen

Achievement   Fulfilment

When working together creates coherence and trust

When working together unites gravitas and excitement

SIGNIFICANCE
How powerful we want to be

Vision   Our Mark

LEGACY
What we want to happen

Engages and inspires. Feels intuitively right

Creates emotional traction for movement forward

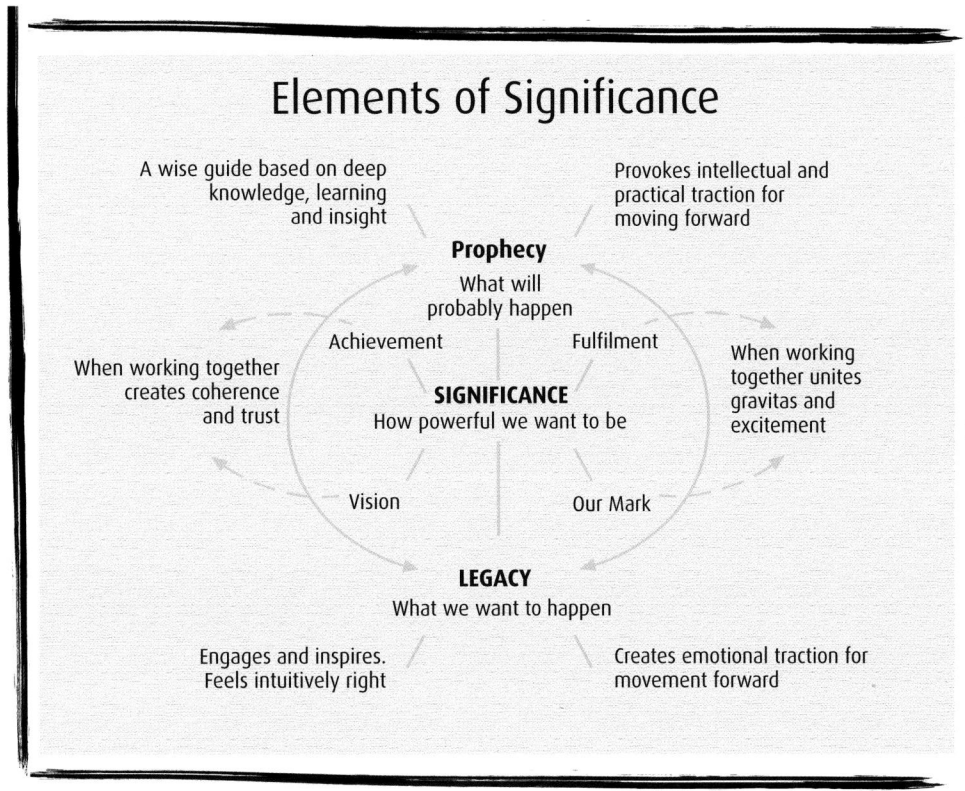

The need for competence (what we do)

The twin paradoxes at the heart of an organisation's or individual's competence are:

The need to be in control of others as well as being controlled by others and secondly the need to learn form others and others learn from us. If these paradoxes are not resolved in useful, innovative ways then the organisation will quickly find itself either delivering sub-standard services/products to an unforgiving market or failing to deliver excellent services or products to the market because of inadequate internal processes. Getting the right degree of control over others and control by others leads away form chaos and rigidity to a sense of order which enables competency to be expressed well. To maximise competence there also needs to be a sweet spot where every constituency learns from every other so that learning builds new order, which builds new learning and so on.

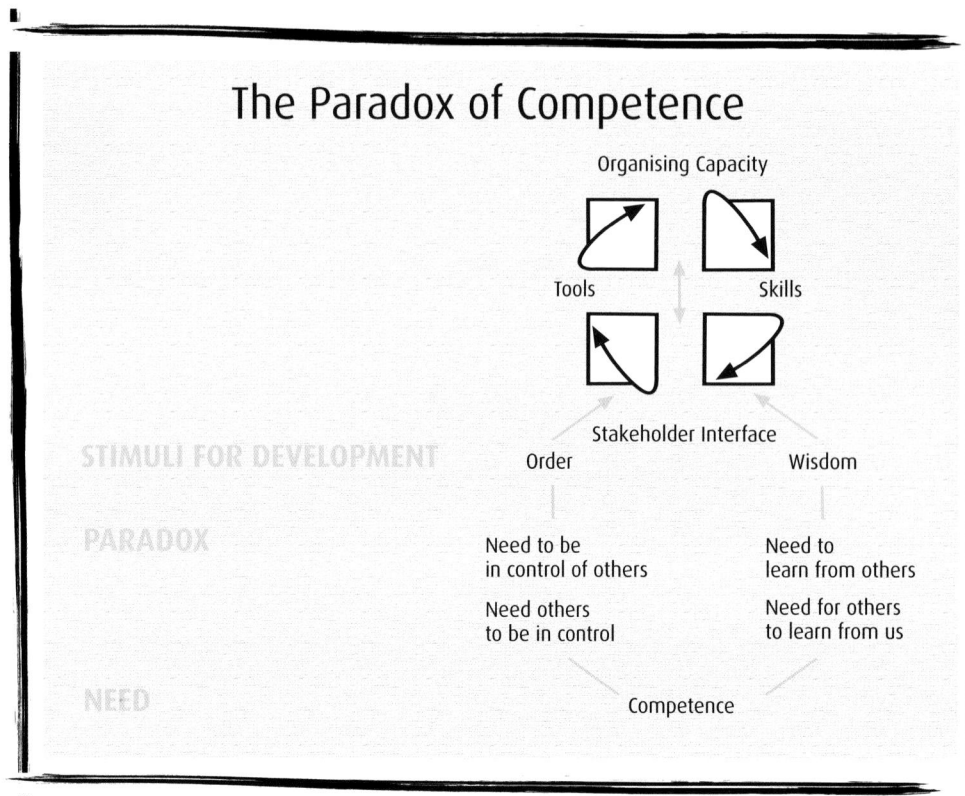

The Paradox of Competence

Organising Capacity

Tools · Skills

Stakeholder Interface

STIMULI FOR DEVELOPMENT

Order · Wisdom

PARADOX

Need to be in control of others · Need to learn from others

Need others to be in control · Need for others to learn from us

NEED

Competence

- The need to control others.

- The need to be controlled by others.

For example, the need for a business leader to control his organisation's destiny while working within mandatory governance regulations; the need for management to free up employees to be individual decision-makers while retaining overall control of their actions; or the need, at an individual level, for a leader to continue to guide the organisation while managing their own departure/retirement.

Resolution here results in some form of order, where roles and responsibilities are clear, decisions are made and the organising elements work together.

The second paradox is:

- The need to learn from others.

- The need for others to learn from us.

When this is resolved usefully, all elements of competence are learning from each other in order to continually build the next level of competence. Wisdom needs to build on wisdom so that the organising capacity is constantly increased to bring new, more effective forms of control to meet changing stakeholder needs.

For example, the need for a management consultancy to be completely in tune with developments in its clients' industry sectors while bringing innovation to all areas of their contact with clients; or the willingness of an internet technology business to work with and learn from its competitors in collaborative industry standards where intellectual property and experience are pooled for the collective good of the sector and/or retailers and manufacturers sharing shopper insights to meet each other's needs.

Resolution of both strands results in organisational capability and an effective stakeholder interface. It equips the organisation and the individual with the tools they need to function effectively.

Elements of Competence

The ability to organise organisational
elements so that the enterprise flourishes

Organising Capacity

Functional and social capabilities needed to meet the goals of the organisation	Skills —— COMPETENCE —— Tools What we do	Machinery hardware and software needed to fulfil the operating plan

Customer Interface
Clicks and Bricks

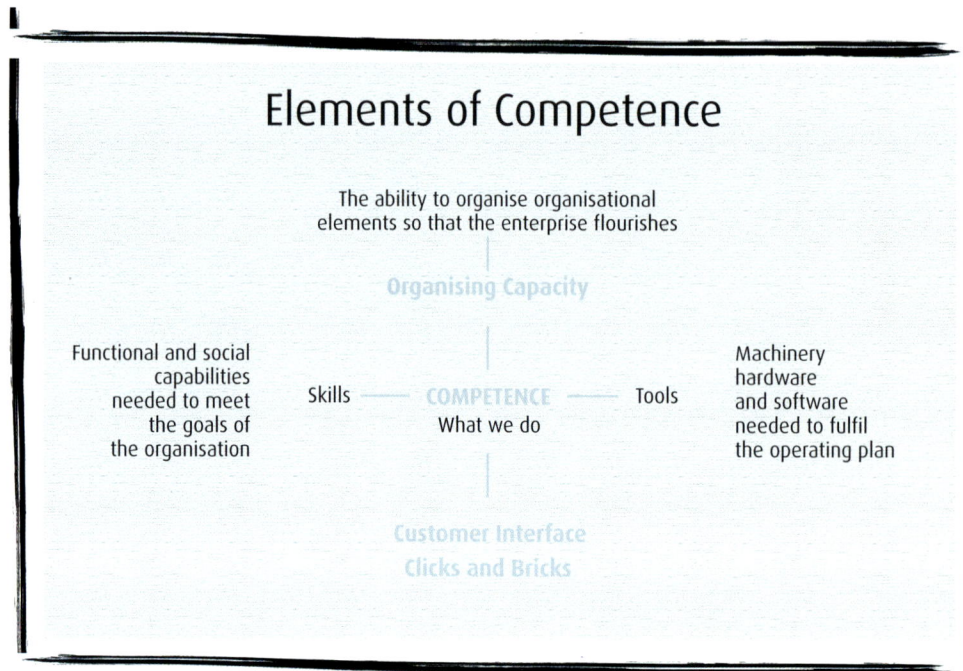

All of the above sets of paradoxes apply equally to individuals and organisations. They are universal. In purely organisational terms, however, other core paradoxes will exist at a deep structure level. These must be understood, assimilated and used creatively and will most probably be a function of the core transactions of the organisation, the motivations of their founders and the significant current needs for change at play in their environment.

DISTINGUISHING FEATURES OF REGENERATION AND CO-CREATION

It is easy, given the complexity and ambiguity of life, to view change as something to be imposed rather than created. Flowing from a belief that change is 'done by the few to the many' is a residual awareness that the majority are powerless to influence the change process and therefore alienation inevitably follows. Change becomes more manageable and less threatening when it is given a cultural fabric and contextualised by past and future changes.

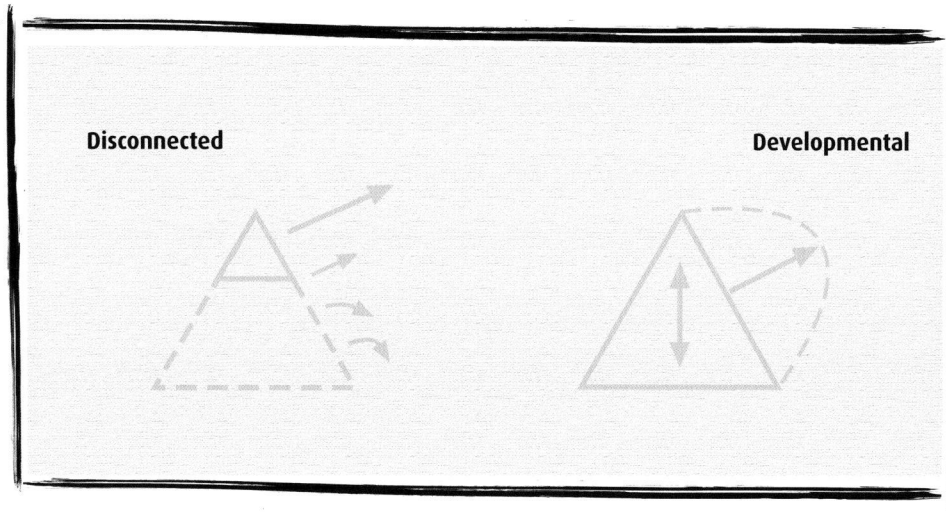

Disconnected | Developmental

Change can also be seen as a lurch from one position to another, events and outcomes are buffeted by global interdependence and volatility. Again, however, change does not need to be disconnected, it can be developmental and pattern can be brought to a chaotic world for short yet essential periods of time. Continually moving, from Muddle to Model to Muddle to Model is precisely what regeneration is about. It provides managed cycles of change that are themselves in time with the rhythms of stakeholder needs.

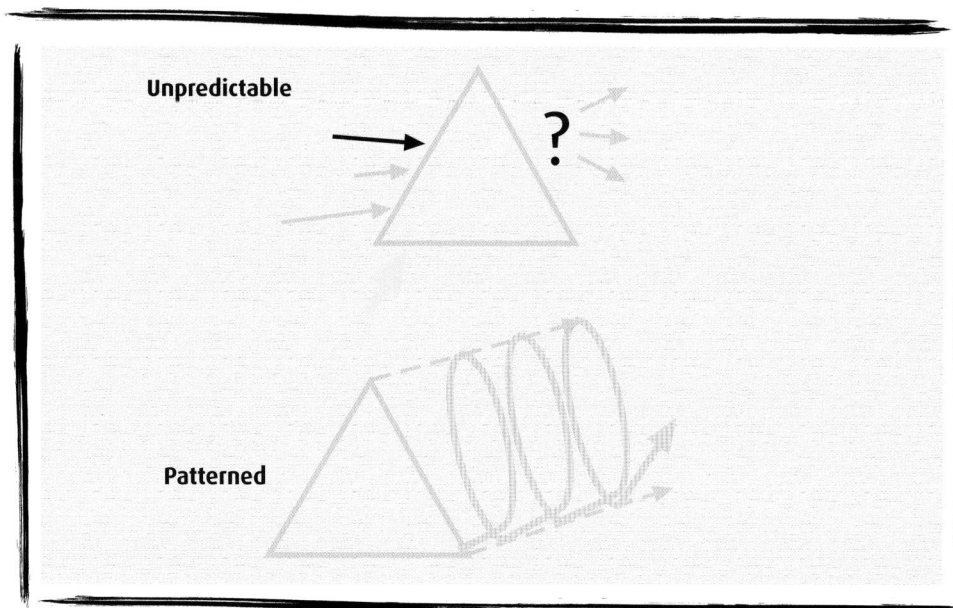

Unpredictable

Patterned

Regeneration and co-creation is different from conventional change and its distinguishing features are:

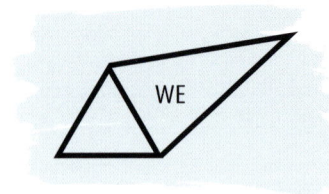

Conventional change	**Regeneration and Co-creation**
US THEM	WE
Hierarchical (them and us)	Shared endeavour (we)

Top-down mechanisms originate from organisation leaders and force change on the rest of the organisation. Regenerative change draws strength from all stakeholders and functions as a collective process.

Burning platform	Managed cycles

Reactive change programmes are often initiated far too late, by creativity rebasing themselves and their organisations before they need to they ensure their future prosperity.

By working through change in managed cycles regeneration avoids the stop/start disruptive effect of reactive change.

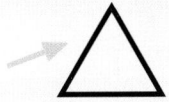

External pressure

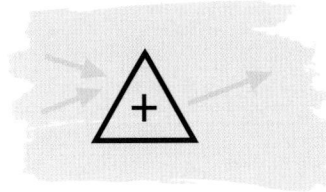

External influences + internal creativity

Conventional change is driven by external pressures. Regenerative change deals with external influences but also does so by drawing on internal creativity.

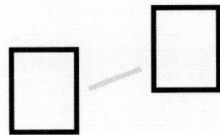

Present – Gap – Future

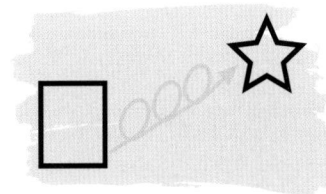

Present – Pattern – Future

Conventional change programmes are designed to move organisations from one competence to another often with little connectivity between the two states. Regenerative change moves organisations forward via managed upward spirals of development of identity, significance, and competence.

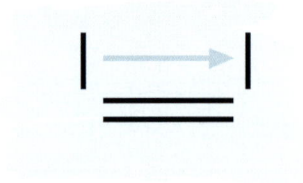

Sequence/Parallel

Coincidence of foreground/background

Change initiatives in many organisations frequently address separate issues in parallel or sequence, instead of drawing these together to maximise their effect. Regenerative change binds background and foreground change agendas to reflect the entirety of the organisation's needs.

Resistance is bad

Resistance needs to be harnessed

Conventional change methodologies identify resistance as a hurdle that must be eradicated/overcome. Regenerative change processes draw strength from the passion and belief that drive heart felt resistance.

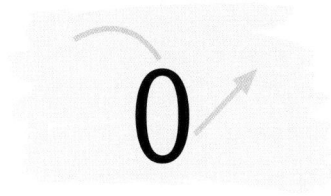

Always starts from zero

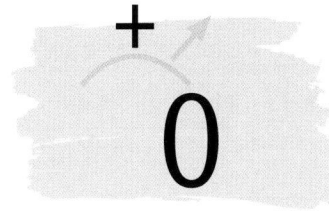

Starts from strength

Regenerative change recognises that you never start again from a zero position. Nothing is ever brand spanking new. In the residual history there will be an amalgam of positive and negative. Taking the positives forward and tuning them enhances the elements that are changed or innovations that are adopted it allows people to notice that their past was not all just junk to be thrown on the scrapheap, that there was gold not just dross and the gold gives the foundation for the future.

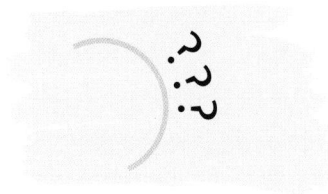

Deals with symptoms

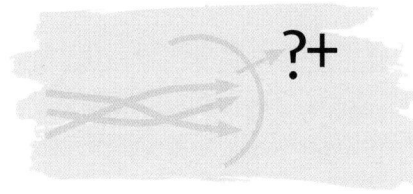

Deals with needs

Reactive change initiatives are implemented by leaders to address specific problems that arise. They do not deal with the 'needs' of the organisation, the root drivers at the tidal level of organisations and the stakeholders' aspirations. Regenerative change does.

$\%$

$\&^2$

Output-oriented   Oriented to outputs, outcomes and legacy.

Most change programmes are designed to address shareholder/stakeholder pressures by boosting short-term measures of productivity. Regenerative change (as an embedded process) develops the entire organisation with improvements to short-term outputs flowing from enhancements to the organisation at a deep-structure, legacy-based level.

T

$T\,T^4$
$T\,T$

Dealing with single 'truths'   Engaging multiple organic 'truths' about the future

Rather than searching for the "single truth" to march toward, regenerative change allows all stakeholders multiple truths to be engaged.

Regeneration is about knitting and unknitting. Building on the patterns and fabrics that were there before to create new ways of thinking and feeling that mesh with the future and create useful action.

REGENERATING SUSTAINABLE CULTURE
Re-jigging the Jigsaw

Cultural regeneration requires periodic stakeholder co-creative conversations, the results of which will be the next iteration of organisation culture that will provide the motive power for new legacy accomplishment. Creativity and compromise ensure cultures are always changing, the challenge is to harness and propel the changes forward.

All organisations are therefore hybrids and undergoing ongoing 'acculturation' process which deliver the prophecy and legacy or not.

The way in which culture is perceived has a strong influence on how it can be changed. Cultures can be interpreted in a range of ways from one dimensional snapshots to multi dimensional ongoing relationship maps.

Culture embodies and springs from a number of different sources; the purpose and nature of the organisations core transactions, any ongoing distinctiveness brought by the founders, current contextual influences, what stakeholders require and the distinctive influencing style of the organisation.

This connected Culture/Brand universe can be seen at a distance as a Mosaic, a discernable profile or zooming in it is seen as a Matrix of organisational structures, processes and behaviours and under closer scrutiny as a Melting Pot, a crucible of complementary and competing needs, instincts, beliefs and assumptions.

Regenerative change and co-creation is achieved by working at the deep structure or Melting Pot level.

PLC MOSAIC

A

MATRIX

x—o—◇ □—o—o □ ◇
◇ □—o—☆—□—□
+—o☆+—o☆ x
+ o—+—o x

A

MELTING POT

!?
↑ ↓
↑ ¿! ↓↑

A

CHOREOGRAPHY FOR THE ONGOING PROFITABLE DANCE OF STAKEHOLDERS CULTURES

CULTURE: JOINING AND MOVING ON

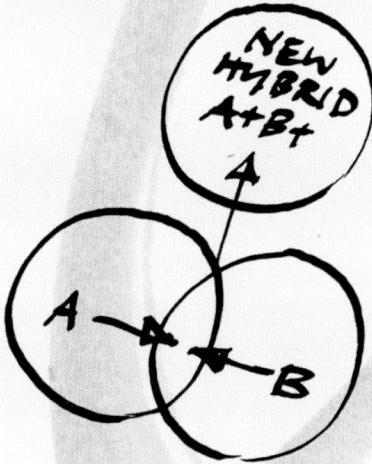

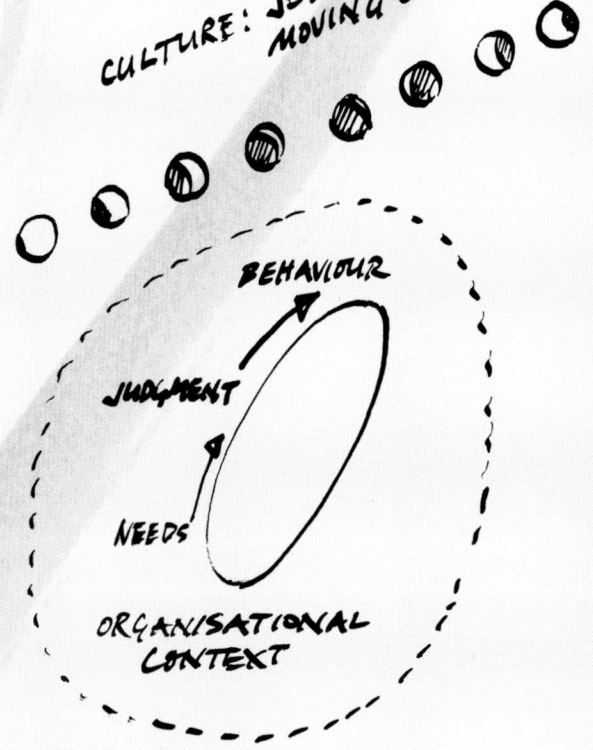

NEW HYBRID A+B+

A

A → B

BEHAVIOUR
JUDGMENT
NEEDS

ORGANISATIONAL CONTEXT

ONE PLUS ONE EQUALS INFINITY

CULTURE CAN BE DIFFERENT BETWEEN DIFFERENT CONSTITUENCIES

RE-JIGGING THE JIGSAW

CULTURE THE SHINE WITHIN

REGENERATING SUSTAINABLE CULTURE –
REJIGGING THE JIGSAW

MOSAIC

Cultural Perspectives

MATRIX

connected Culture

MELTING POT

MAYBE

YES

Cultures -
Joining and Moving On

NO

Acculturation

REGENERATING SUSTAINABLE CULTURE
Rejigging the jigsaw

Building the appropriate culture to meet stakeholder needs is the key to the leader's quest for regenerating the value of the organisation's assets and relationships. This focus underpins the cycle of constant change and improvement that is needed to inject innovation and creativity into the processes, products and services with which the organisation strives to meet stakeholder needs.

The ability and courage to take their organisation's culture forward is a continuous prerequisite for leaders. Instead of having their time just taken up with the instantaneous wishes and immediate wants that can dominate day-to-day organisational life, leaders must balance their attention between these short-term drivers and the long-term needs which will define the organisation's future internal condition. By being willing and able to define the fundamental aspirations that drive their own performance (their own individual culture) and the organisation's culture, their short-term decision-making will move into alignment with long-term strategic prophecy.

Successful cultural regeneration requires a series of conversations that leaders and their teams have with all their stakeholders. These will define the always changing 'shine within' which enables the organisation to be always relevant and slightly ahead of its time.

Culture change is not as simple as denoting 'good' and 'bad' cultures and ordering a shift from the latter to the former. Successful cultures are ones with the best fit to prophecy, strategies and priorities. There is no 'one size fits all' where culture is concerned. Cultures are always changing, the challenge is to harness and propel the changes forward. Cultures can't be usefully changed by email and diktat, any change is a collective relationship process requiring commitment, time and effort from the leadership throughout the organisation and stakeholder's universe.

Most definitions of culture envision it as a fixed state: 'This is how we do things round here.' This is a misinterpretation of how things really are. All organisations are hybrids and undergoing an ongoing 'acculturation' process, their cultures are continuously in flux. At every moment, regardless of the size, scope, location or composition of an organisation, compromise and innovative activities are always taking place and every single interaction changes the next reality of culture for the organisation. These will be a mixture of minute evolutionary and large revolutionary shifts. Even trying to stop a culture from changing changes the culture. A slight change in the way the phone is answered, a fundamental shift in the reward system and the introduction of rules to enforce a consistent culture all prompt the acculturation process. The challenge for leaders is to regenerate the culture so that its internal Identity (Culture) works in tandem with its external Identity (Brand) to achieve the Significance that the organisation and their stakeholders aspire to.

Acculturation

Organisational cultures are continuously adapted by - and adapting to - the various ongoing stakeholder interactions that take place inside and outside the organisation.

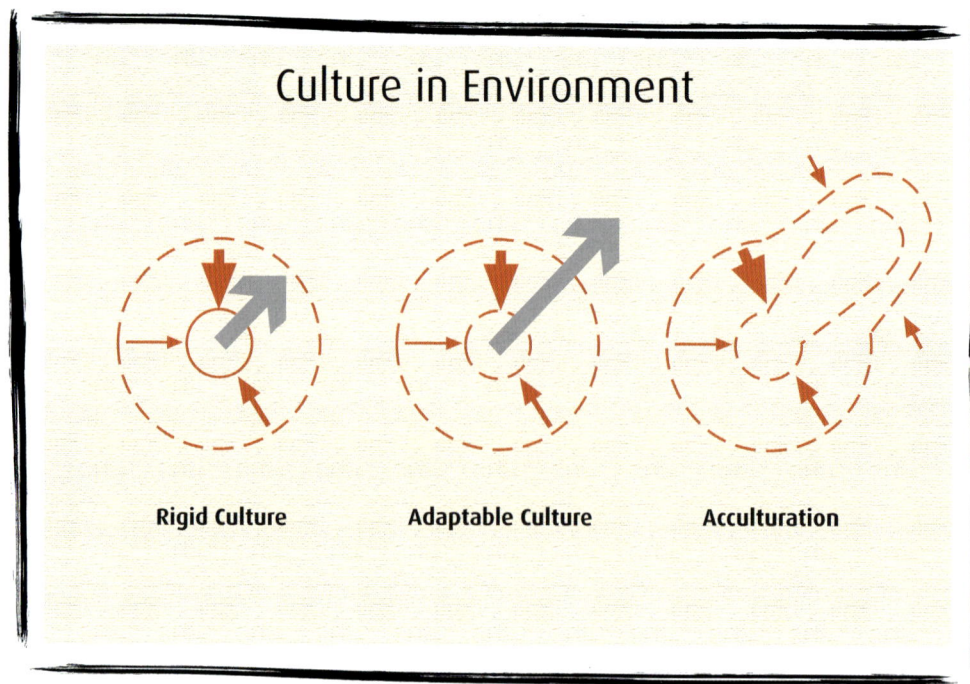

Culture in Environment

Rigid Culture   Adaptable Culture   Acculturation

Organisational cultures will always adapt to some degree to the environment in which they find themselves. It is, however, important for leaders to contain or expand that level of adaptation according to their stakeholder needs. Leaders must accept that a level of granular and ongoing adaptation is always there and that they are also responsible for the propulsion of the planned 'weeding and seeding' process of acculturation.

Having permeable boundaries between stakeholders will allow and enable useful acculturation conversations to take place. A **rigid** culture is one that allows limited opportunity for 'tainting' of its present right and wrong ways of being and doing and thus limits its capacity for growth. An **adaptable** culture is one that encourages conversations across its boundaries to ensure that its short to medium term goals are met by appropriate changes in culture. Acculturation happens when all stakeholders are engaged with the continual design/build of new ways of doing and being that ensure an organisation flourishes over time.

Wherever two or more cultures (individuals, organisations, nationalities) meet, an opportunity for acculturation occurs, there will be a latent capacity for all to build something new drawing upon the best of the others. However, if this opportunity is missed, something is lost and the interaction becomes in some way deficient. For example in a failed merger/takeover, or the breakdown of an arms or peace treaty or the collapse of a franchisee/franchisor relationship.

For acculturation to take place adequately there must be a real sense of what the organisation **has** and **is** and **can** and **will** be in terms of its identity, significance and competence. If that sense is anything other than solid, resolved and understood then it will be hard to bring about the next useful culture/hybrid, so the internal condition of the organisation will not optimally satisfy the legitimate needs of its stakeholders.

CULTURE PERSPECTIVES

The way in which culture is perceived and understood has a strong influence on how it can be changed and what it can be changed to.

Cultures can be interpreted in a number of ways:

- One-dimensional snapshots.
- Bi-polar two dimensional fixes.
- Strategic two-dimensional maps of the present and the future.
- Multi-dimensional relationship journeys leading to ongoing regeneration.

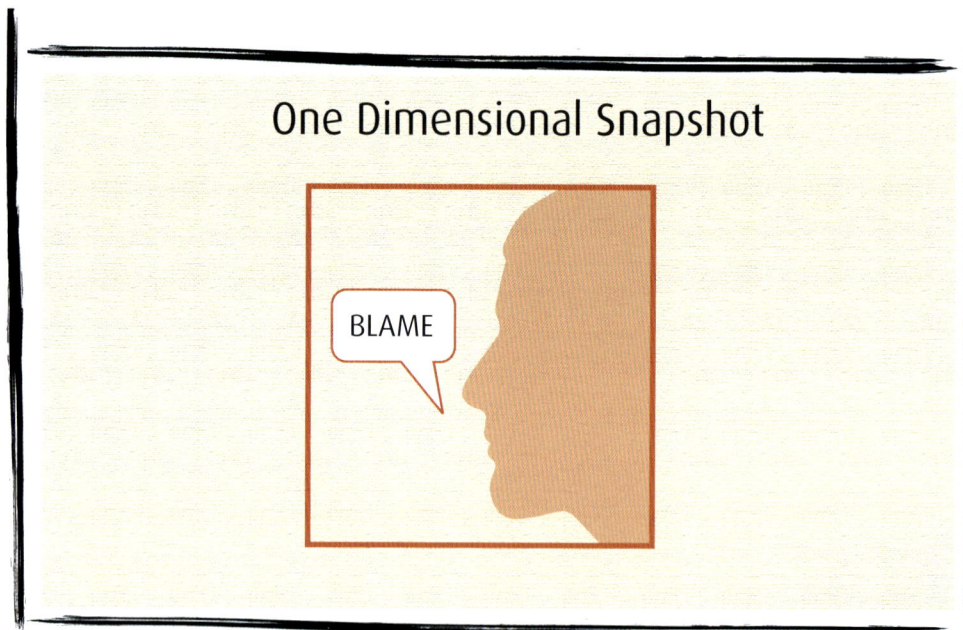

One-dimensional view of organisational culture

This is a simple profile of what is or what you want to be - a snapshot of an organisation's present and/or future culture rather than an in-depth analysis of internal and external manifestations. For example, "a blame culture", "a profit culture" or "a shareholder value culture". Changes here would be from one fixed point to another.

Two-dimensional tactical choices

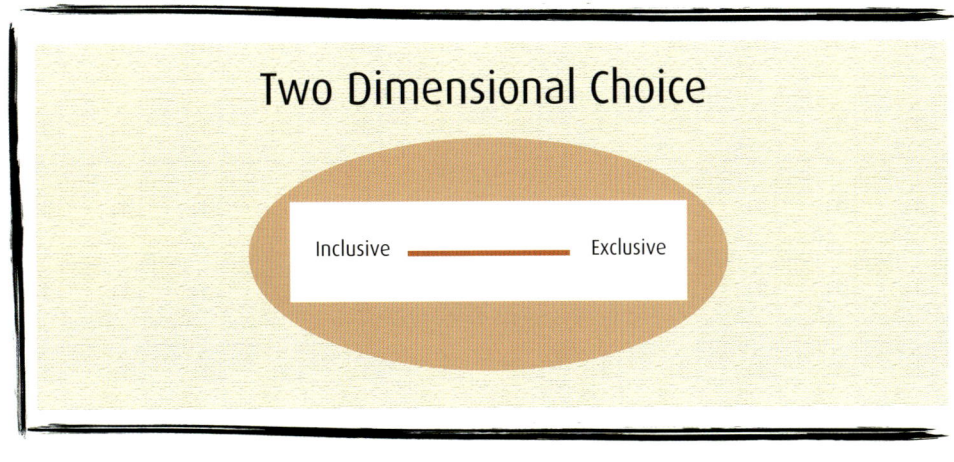

A geographical 'fix' on precisely where the organisation's culture falls between any two extremes and where you would like it to move to. For example, is it more collegiate than individualistic? This interpretation recognises that every organisation faces certain fundamental choices when it comes to culture but limits the possibility of integrating the best of both poles of the chosen characteristics.

Strategic interpretation - two-dimensional mapping the culture

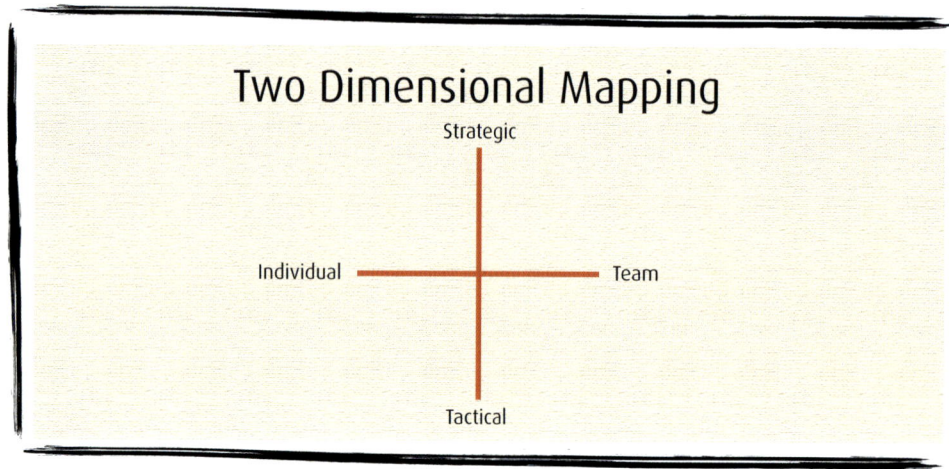

Two Dimensional Mapping

Strategic

Individual ———— ┼ ———— Team

Tactical

This interpretation provides a 'route-map' for organisations and their leaders. Instead of simply 'fixing' the culture at a given point and providing another fix to move forward, this enables leaders to plot where they need to move the organisation towards. A point between two dimensions of choice in different sets of conditions. So that in an organisations manufacturing environment you might plan for a tactically oriented strong team ethos, whereas, in a fund raising function you might aspire to a strategic, individualistic culture.

Regenerative interpretation

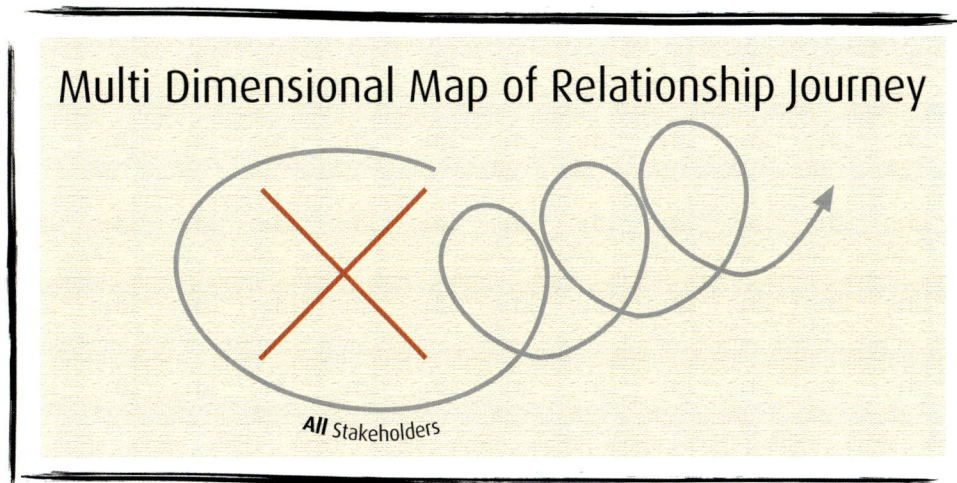

Multi Dimensional Map of Relationship Journey

All Stakeholders

The most sophisticated of all, this interpretation provides a three-dimensional representation of the organisation's culture in relation to its stakeholders. This relational map can only be co-created with stakeholders and has to enable the useful resolution of their differentiated needs.

Here the culture embodies and assimilates all the extremes of which it is comprised. It is also in a continuous process of change as it adapts to its surrounding environment, one which it relates with freely, rather than being isolated from external stakeholders. To flourish via this model organisations must remain open to acculturation processes drawing strength from the regenerative change that they are experiencing. Each part of the organisation will always be moving toward a culture that satisfies their particular stakeholders configuration of needs. Given that stakeholding is an interdependent process then any regeneration of an organisations culture should always result in a change in the stakeholders culture. So, this multi-dimensional mapping is the choreography for the ongoing profitable dance of all stakeholders future cultures. In this way it is possible for an airline alliance to have a number of nationalities and a mix of the alliance members' staff as stewards on the same flight to deal with the diverse needs springing from their customers' cultures; or for a car finance company to have different ways of doing business when working across a variety of motor manufacturers from different continents, focussing on the particular stakeholders needs, rather than the generic industry grouping.

Ironically, taking a snapshot or holding a bi-polar view of culture is not a useful way of simplifying, instead it accommodates long-held beliefs leaving them less open to change. Political correctness adopts a flat, static stance which stifles change. It makes it possible to say that certain actions are only right and only wrong. Taking two and multi dimensional views of culture allows for change as well as including the capacity to say things are right(ish) or wrong(ish) in the never ending culture transitions. An organisation can therefore be flexible enough to co-create a number of different hybrid cultures depending on the significance and nature of the stakeholder relationship and the legacy that the parties are trying to create together. Culture can be different for different constituencies.

At the same time there will also be a need to differentiate culture so that an organisation is seen to be distinct in the manner in which it adds value across all of its stakeholder relationships. The consistent gold thread that characterises all of its stakeholder relationships. Other sources of differentiation include any heritage left by the founders of the organisation, the purpose and nature of core transactions, the current contextual issues facing the organisation and the style which characterises the way the organisation gets things done.

The persona of the founding individual or groups can have a very long afterlife. If this is useful to meeting current and future stakeholder needs then these cultural elements should be fostered and amplified.

The nature of the organisation's purpose and the core transactions that it pursues with and for its stakeholders also determines the culture and the needs, values, instincts and behaviours that exemplify it. It seems self evident that pharmaceutical companies should care, auditors should be cautious, retailers should serve, banks should be fiscally responsible, a civil service should promote a civil society. However, in reality, this often is not the case.

The other element that culture has to embody is the medium term context that the organisation and its leaders exist in. So that culture should help address for example, a food retailers view on sustainable farming, a food manufacturers stance on obesity, a pharmaceutical company's view on the commoditisation of what formally were propriety therapies and an airline's plans for how to deal with its carbon footprint.

Once the organisation's culture contains and embodies the purpose and nature of the core transactions, the ongoing founder's voice, the contextual influences and the differentiated satisfaction of stakeholder's needs then the question of the distinctive manner in which culture serves the organisation and its stakeholders becomes live.

How judgment is brought to the manner in which culture serves its stakeholders will provide this added differentiation. The judgment is brought to the behaviour options that the resolution of the needs for Identity, Significance, and Competence throw up.

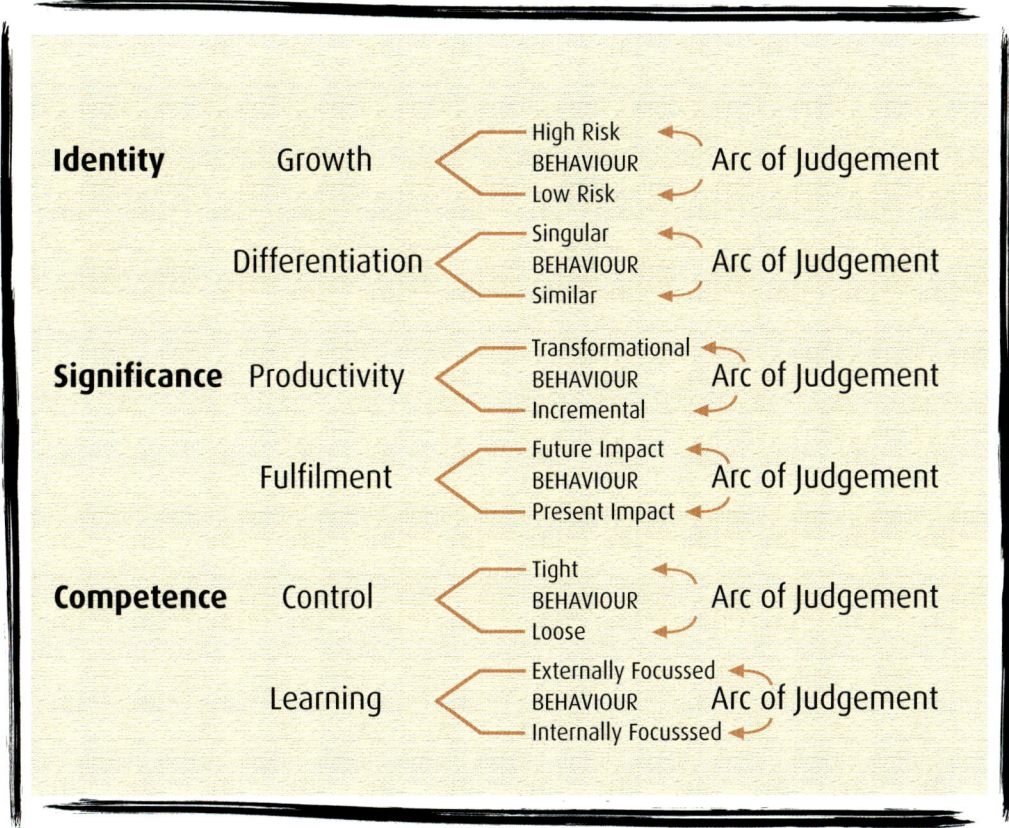

Identity	Growth	High Risk / BEHAVIOUR / Low Risk	Arc of Judgement
	Differentiation	Singular / BEHAVIOUR / Similar	Arc of Judgement
Significance	Productivity	Transformational / BEHAVIOUR / Incremental	Arc of Judgement
	Fulfilment	Future Impact / BEHAVIOUR / Present Impact	Arc of Judgement
Competence	Control	Tight / BEHAVIOUR / Loose	Arc of Judgement
	Learning	Externally Focussed / BEHAVIOUR / Internally Focusssed	Arc of Judgement

So for each stakeholder it is possible to bring, on top of the core culture descriptors, a judgment about the kind of behaviours most suited to the mutual satisfaction of the particular stakeholder groupings' needs.

So, with a key supplier with a track record of slow, intermittent delivery you might judge to adopt a behaviour profile that is low risk, present impact, tight control and singular. With a shareholder with concerns about volatility in their investment portfolio a judgment to behave in a low risk similar, incremental manner, with tight control might be a sound judgment. However, with a shareholder with medium term needs for high returns your behaviour might be higher risk, singular and transformational. With a regulator your behavioural profile would probably be internally focused, tight control, similar to others in the industry and low risk behaviour.

So, at its most useful the internal Identity of an organisation, its culture, should embody and enable the nature of its purpose and core transactions, the useful distinctiveness brought by its founders, its stand on medium term contextual influences, the differentiated satisfaction of stakeholder needs and the style it brings to the manner on which it satisfies those needs.

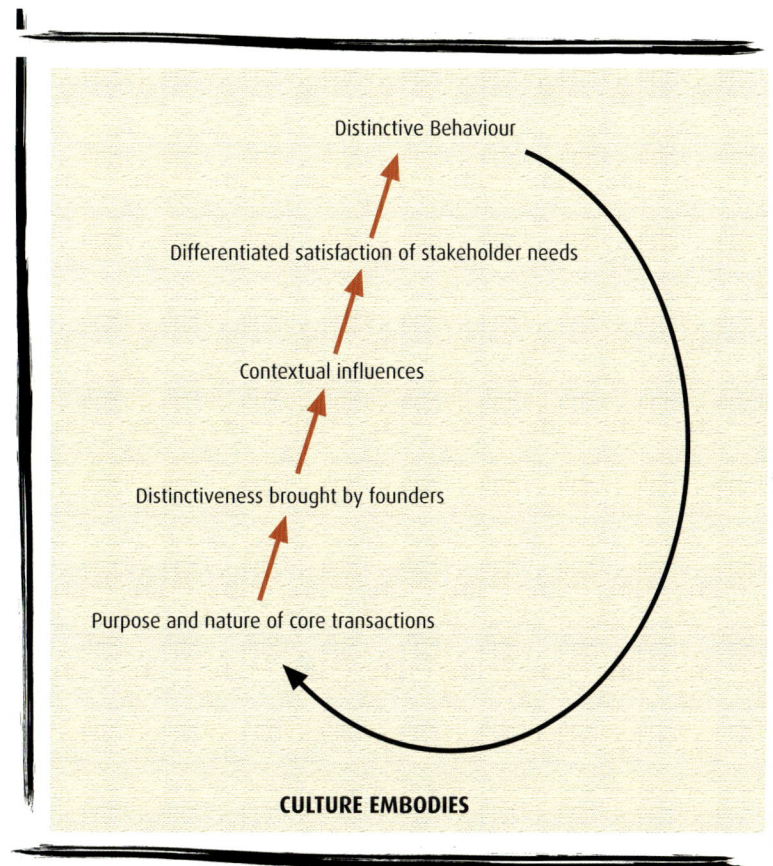

Distinctive Behaviour

Differentiated satisfaction of stakeholder needs

Contextual influences

Distinctiveness brought by founders

Purpose and nature of core transactions

CULTURE EMBODIES

This is an iterative cycle and at best is embodied in the Brand and Culture in order to provide clear identity which will be attractive, compelling and create loyalty from and with all stakeholder constituencies.

CONNECTED CULTURES

Identity can only be seen in relationships with others; nothing exists or flourishes on its own. The inner manifestation of an organisation is its culture and the outer is its brand, in the same way individuals have an inner world and outer representation. When the individual's and the organisation's Identity are connected and in sync then the energy builds from one to the other. Delivering a significant legacy becomes more likely.

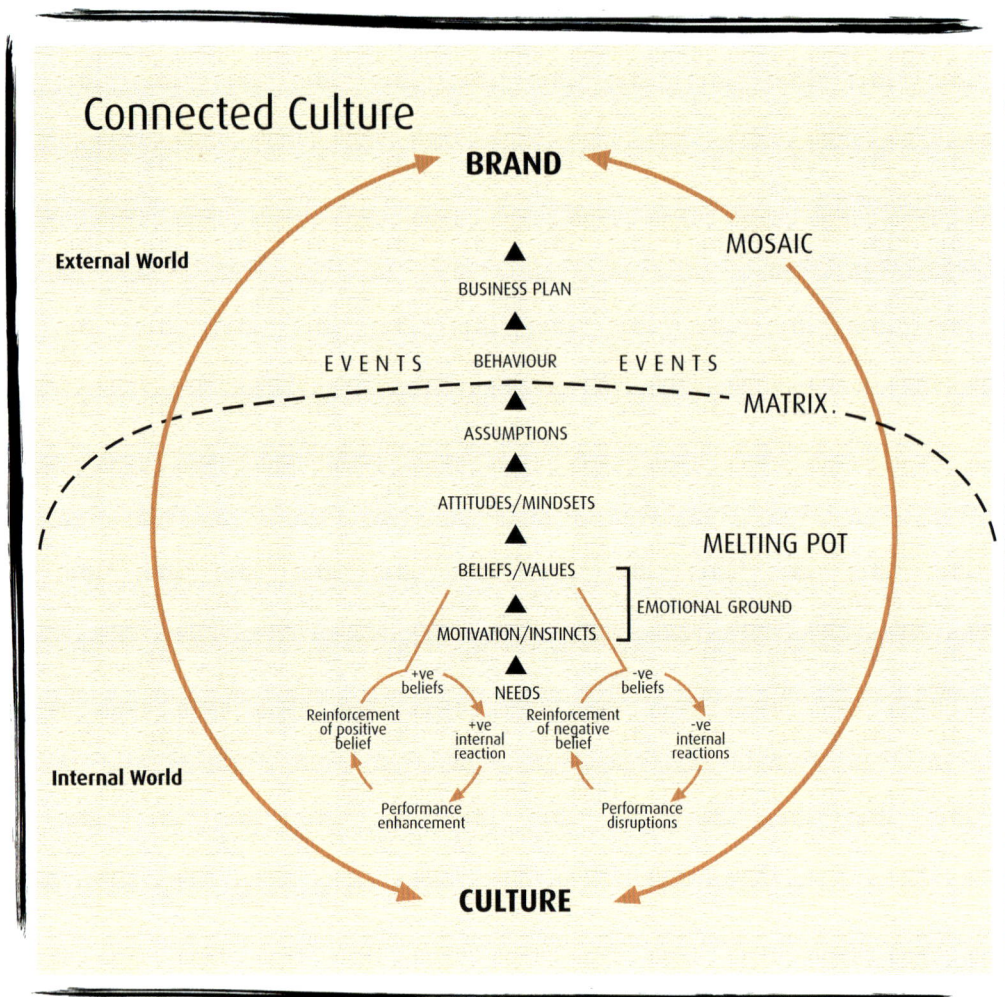

Connected Culture

BRAND

External World

MOSAIC

▲

BUSINESS PLAN

▲

EVENTS   BEHAVIOUR   EVENTS

MATRIX.

▲

ASSUMPTIONS

▲

ATTITUDES/MINDSETS

MELTING POT

▲

BELIEFS/VALUES

▲   EMOTIONAL GROUND

MOTIVATION/INSTINCTS

▲

+ve beliefs   NEEDS   -ve beliefs

Reinforcement of positive belief   +ve internal reaction   Reinforcement of negative belief   -ve internal reactions

Internal World

Performance enhancement   Performance disruptions

CULTURE

The Connected Nature of Culture

Understanding an organisation's and an individual's culture means understanding the ongoing dance/journey it has with its stakeholder environment, as well as understanding its internal dynamics which change to dictate its relevance. The diagram depicts identity showing its external influence, its brand manifestation as well as its internal dynamic composition - its culture.

Needs and Instincts connect culture

This way of understanding a connected culture can be viewed from three perspectives depending on the distance you view them from. From the widest angle lens connected culture will be seen as a mosaic, a near enough homogenised whole. As you zoom closer you become aware of the matrix that makes up the mosaic, the connections, the similarities and the differences in practice, procedure, assumption and mindsets that determine what happens and what doesn't. When you focus in to close up you become aware of the melting pot of dilemmas and paradoxes, the points of choice that occur in the deep structure of an organisation where similar complementary and competing beliefs, motivations, instincts and needs are thrown together and need some form of resolution. These are the underground springs of creative possibility and stagnant pools of poor habits ingrained over generations which are in dynamic tension and need to be given attention if acculturation is to be beneficial.

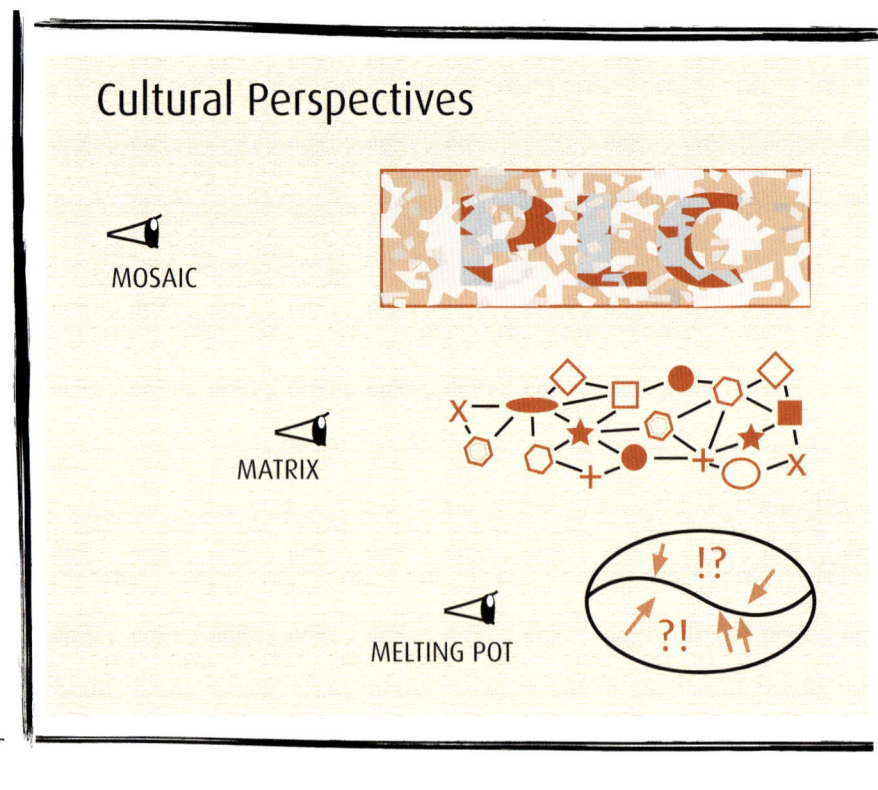

Cultural Perspectives

MOSAIC

MATRIX

MELTING POT

Mosaic/Motif

MOSAIC

Looked at from a distance, organisational cultures are broad-brush mosaics embodied, ideally, in the brands that set them apart from their competitors. These brands should embody the needs, instincts, customs and values of the organisations they represent.

At this range, most same-sector organisations appear to be doing the same thing. There is little light and shade. Indeed, at this level, even fundamentally dysfunctional organisations can project integrity. An organisation's brand and market capability may never be in doubt until its sudden implosion. But closer inspection would have shown that its values were not being reflected in its behaviours.

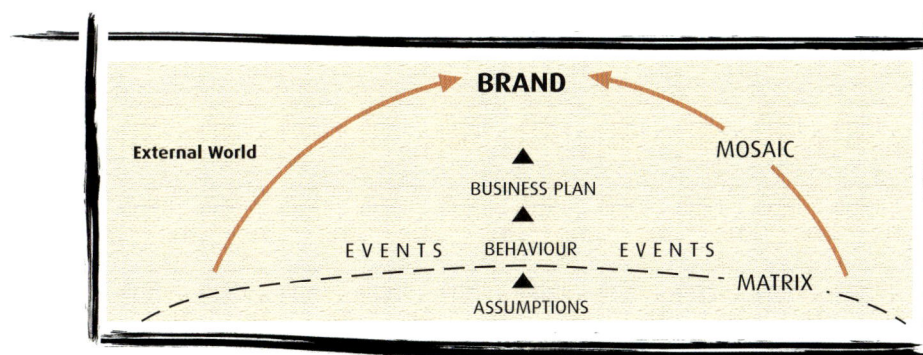

BRAND

External World

MOSAIC

▲
BUSINESS PLAN
▲
E V E N T S   BEHAVIOUR   E V E N T S
▲
ASSUMPTIONS

MATRIX

Matrix

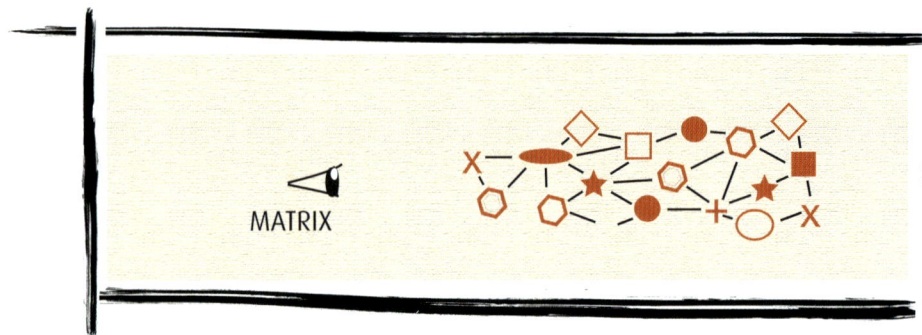

MATRIX

Zooming in, the mosaic begins to separate into matrices of organisational behaviours as the processes and structures employed come into sharper focus. At this level, the attitudes, mindsets and assumptions that colour behaviour and therefore cultures come into relief. The interaction between these elements can be identified and analysed to determine if they are working together in ways which satisfy stakeholder needs.

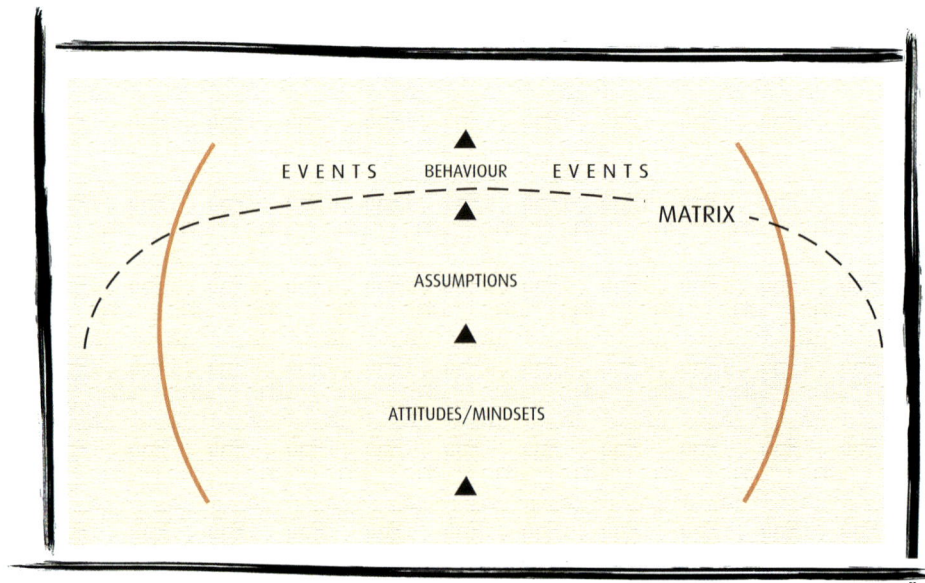

EVENTS   BEHAVIOUR   EVENTS   MATRIX

ASSUMPTIONS

ATTITUDES/MINDSETS

Melting Pot

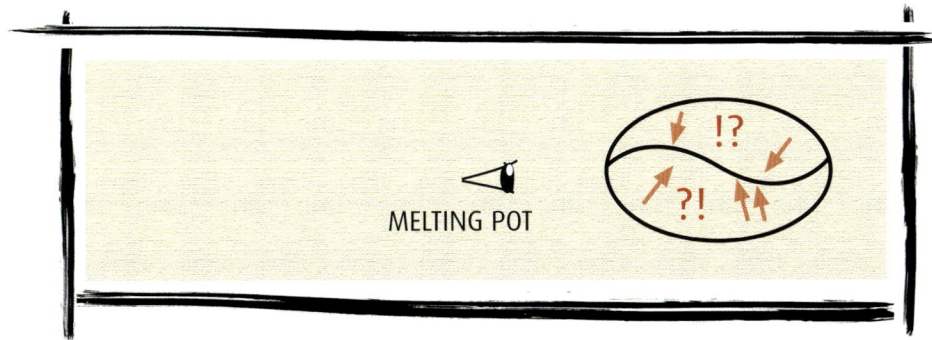

MELTING POT

Underlying these matrices, at a deep structure level within the organisation are needs, beliefs, values, motivations and instincts played out either as negative or virtuous cycles of thought and feeling. These feed into - and dictate - how the organisation's regenerative or degenerative journey continues. The negative degenerative cycle is when a distorted belief system fuels performance disruption which, in turn, results in diminished capability and outcomes. A virtuous, regenerative cycle is when the organisational culture is continually validated resulting in positive belief, confident mindsets and performance enhancement. These cycles which play such an important part in shaping and directing organisational culture are the responsibility of leaders. They are covered more fully in the Leading Regeneration section. The leader's duty is to monitor these, assess their impact and, where appropriate, initiate deep-structure change geared to rejuvenate and revivify the culture. Doing so effectively means developing an understanding of the paradoxes that lie at the heart of every organisation and accepting that there are only rightish or wrongish answers. Effective leaders manage to view their organisations in a 'relational' context rather than forcing their interpretation to coincide with convenient 'fixed points'. Regenerative leadership implies an ability to assimilate contradiction - and draw strength from it.

Regenerative change is achieved by working at the deep-structure or Melting Pot level. It is here that the quest to build and transform the value of an organisation and its assets begins.

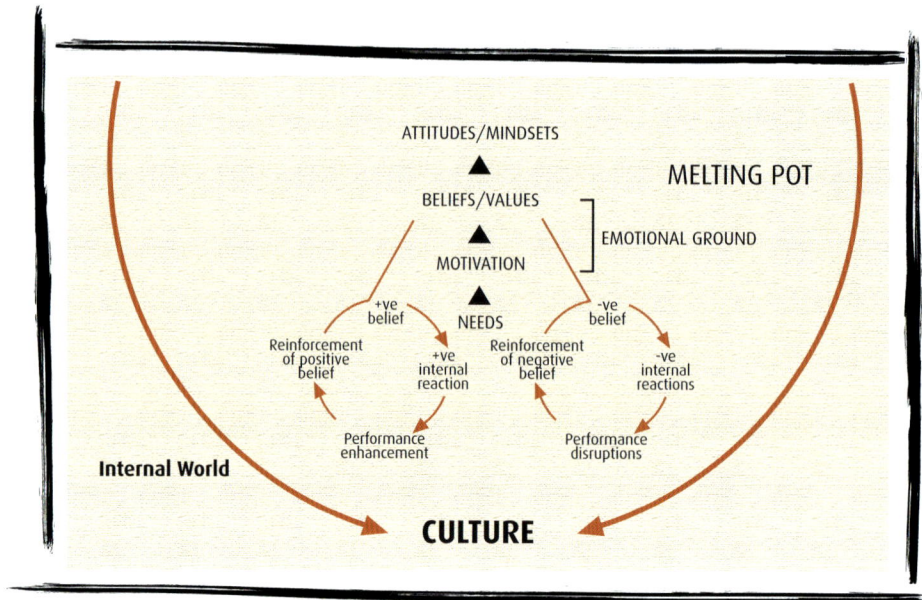

By initiating and sustaining the appropriate stakeholder conversations leaders become capable of fulfilling their primary function, identifying and regenerating the patterns and cycles and, the needs, values, beliefs and motivations that lie at the heart of all their stakeholders' cultures.

THE ACCULTURATION CYCLE

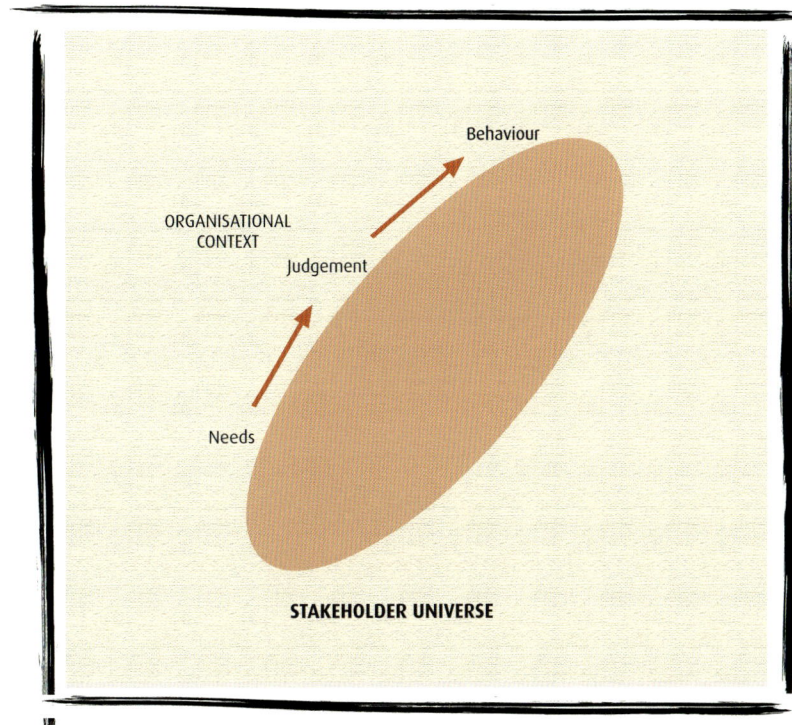

Developing cultures – needs, judgment and behaviour

For any organisation, culture is the product of the interaction between the three core elements that make up the Culture Circle. The diagram above exemplifies the way in which an organisation's **culture** both shapes - and is shaped by - the **needs**, **judgments** and **behaviours** underpinning it. These same needs and behaviours are themselves shaped by the judgments (internal and external) governing the organisation's existence. The stories that are told and remembered in organisations are the stories of clear success and obvious failure of these elements to align and build on each other or not.

Needs

Organisational needs are one of the core components of organisational culture. A need is a deep rooted itch that demands to be scratched in order for the organisation to survive and flourish.

The current nature of these often paradoxical needs, the choices and the dilemmas they throw up and, how they can be resolved is the co-creative conversation necessary for effective culture to be continually regenerated.

A need is not the same as a value. Values are very important and stem from needs, however, they have become static statements of principle rather than dynamic guides to action. For instance, a company can say it values growth but nevertheless retains a need to protect what it has; say that it values diversity but still hires people in its own image.

More important, values impose a binary, black-and-white view of the world: an action is either in line with values, or not. In this sense, values can fail to recognise the complexity of the world and of organisational life.

Behaviour

People believe their eyes as well as their ears. What people actually do in an organisation is the most obvious expression of its culture. Even small acts or statements can have a profound influence on the culture of a team, department or organisation. Behaviour obviously influences and is influenced by organisational needs: for example, a company with a need to be inclusive is less likely to behave in a discriminatory fashion. In terms of culture, expecting and maintaining certain standards of behaviour is vital whatever the underlying prejudices of the individual. Behaviour is a key lever for changing cultures and all too often, of course, organisations have professed values, missions, statements, principles saying one thing and behaviour patterns saying exactly the opposite.

Judgments

Judgments are expressed in the rules, protocols and procedures of an organisation. They reflect what is acceptable and not in relation to all stakeholder relationships. Procedures reflect, define and encourage the judgments of an organisation. Of course, if an organisation succeeds in making the right judgments instinctively the rules, protocols and procedures become less important in day-to-day interaction, while continuing to provide a solid floor to operate upon. So a measure of success in embedding useful judgment into culture is the infrequency with which rules are invoked.

Paradoxical needs underpin an organisation's culture and provide the key to its understanding. Cultures are defined by how they resolve these paradoxical needs with each stakeholder. Changing these at a deep structure, 'melting pot' level, will result in changes to the judgments and behaviour and therefore the culture and the brand and in this way the next iteration of Identity is formed.

Any culture is, at its heart, a combination of paradoxes with light and shadow both represented. Where these contrapuntal forces are resolved usefully the organisation's culture will carry latent positive potential within it. Finding this effective resolution will bring the appropriate stakeholder connection, affection, loyalty and love to the culture and the brand.

However, where part of the paradox is overused, the culture can become unbalanced, lapsing into anomie. Needs are ignored, instincts go haywire, motivations turn sour; the organisation begins to lose its compass.

The crucial issue is to bring the appropriate needs, instincts, values, attitudes and behaviour to the boundary of their contact to their stakeholders. Some of these elements will be appropriate for all stakeholders over fairly long periods of time, potentially forever, as they underpin not just what differentiates you, but also your license to operate. Honesty, after all, would appear to be a fairly mandatory universal element for cultures. Some of the elements of culture will be more ephemeral, necessary for one particular business or relationship journey cycle. So, having a keen internal focus after a health and safety incident or, when engaged in a price war to focus all your behaviour on singularly differentiating your product or service on anything rather than price would be a useful judgment.

It is vital not to get too comfortable with the culture you operate in. External forces act on culture so even without an overt intervention the culture is changing. Discomforting the culture through planned regeneration means that there is a lot more control of the emerging hybrid and it is far more likely to serve future needs than just accommodate yesterday's and today's events.

CULTURES, JOINING AND MOVING ON

This ongoing regeneration of culture is different from the potentially more dramatic regeneration at first contact with new cultures and in the separation of what was once a whole entity an established culture. This would include takeovers, mergers, joint ventures, buy ins/outs, turnarounds, spin offs and demergers. The opportunity in the first contact case is to co-create a hybrid culture from two or more entities that have had no prior significant history together. The opportunity from separation is to do it in such a way that the best of the previous culture is brought to the creation of the next hybrid.

The degree of contact and the permeability of the boundaries at the joining phase between the new relationships is vital. One extreme is to ensure that there is no cultural contact at all. In this case, say in, a private equity's or holding group's portfolio of companies, it may be important that there is no cross contamination of the cultures both between the new acquisition and the holding company and the other companies within the portfolio, each should be allowed to regenerate a culture suitable to their own core transactions, legacy and heritage, stakeholder needs and current needs for adaption. Each discreet entity of the portfolio might need a strong cultural shake up perhaps instigated by a new leadership team; this however would be of no concern to other assets in the portfolio.

When there is seen to be a need for two or more once separate entities to function as one with their own distinct set of stakeholders then at the cusp between moving on from the old and joining together with the new there should be highly permeable boundaries and deep cultural contact. This can only be done if both parties understand the deep structure and the interdependent connectivity of their existing cultures all the way up from the deepest needs, instincts, values and motivations through their behaviour, to the practical manifestation of their brand. Most parties in mergers and acquisition spend very little time on cultural due diligence and a lot of mergers and acquisitions sub optimise and fail because of cultural malfunctions.

If both parties have a sophisticated understanding of their Identity (Culture ↔ Brand) as well as the normally more understood Significance (potential future performance) and Competence (what they do well/badly) the ensuing dialogue becomes meaningful and informed judgment can be made in all areas of organisational life. It's important to remember there will always be a culture whether anything is done to regenerate it or not and the culture infects everything so it's an oversight to ignore culture, it's a key factor in the success of any merger, acquisition, joint venture, or buy in/buy out.

Cultural Due Diligence

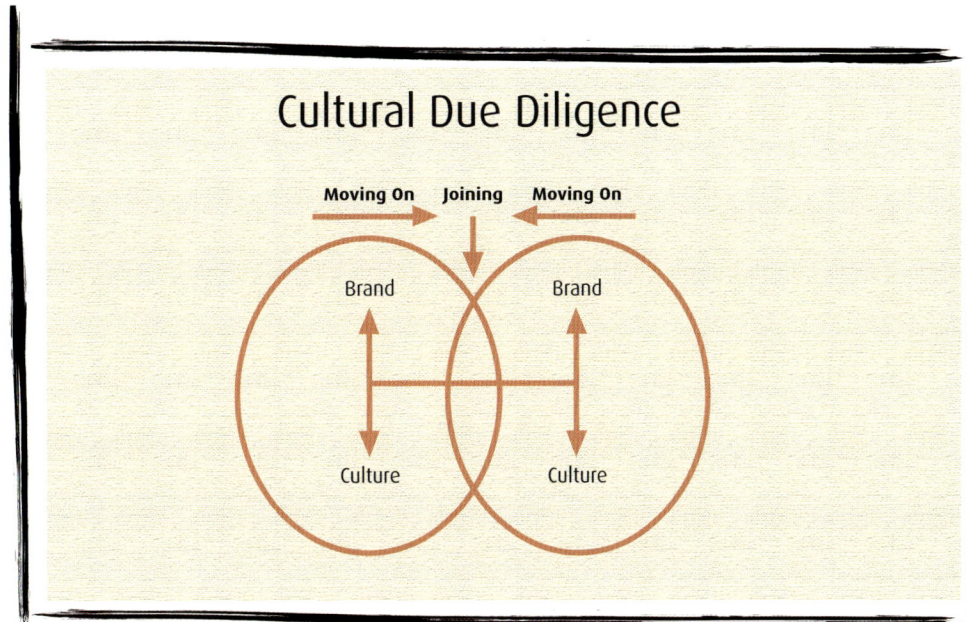

Cultural Breakdown

Where both cultures have not understood or explored cultural due diligence and there has been no, or limited, flow through of meaningful cultural information at the melting pot level then the merged space contains limited benefit and no potential for sustainable growth. Both cultures remain self contained at a mosaic or matrix level and synergies are notably absent. The result is the newly 'joined' organisations become stuck in time, energy is dissipated and at the extreme Anomie sets in and the organisation could lose its commercial, social and ethical compass. Mergers and acquisitions that go this route don't normally last. For a few months or a few years the lack of synergy, the lack of a melting pot, can be glossed over. Inevitably however, rejection sets in and the parties will move on to their next future but worse off than when they first met. So much energy has been put in to trying to join the 'foreign bodies' together at the wrong level that it would have probably been better if they hadn't come together in the first place.

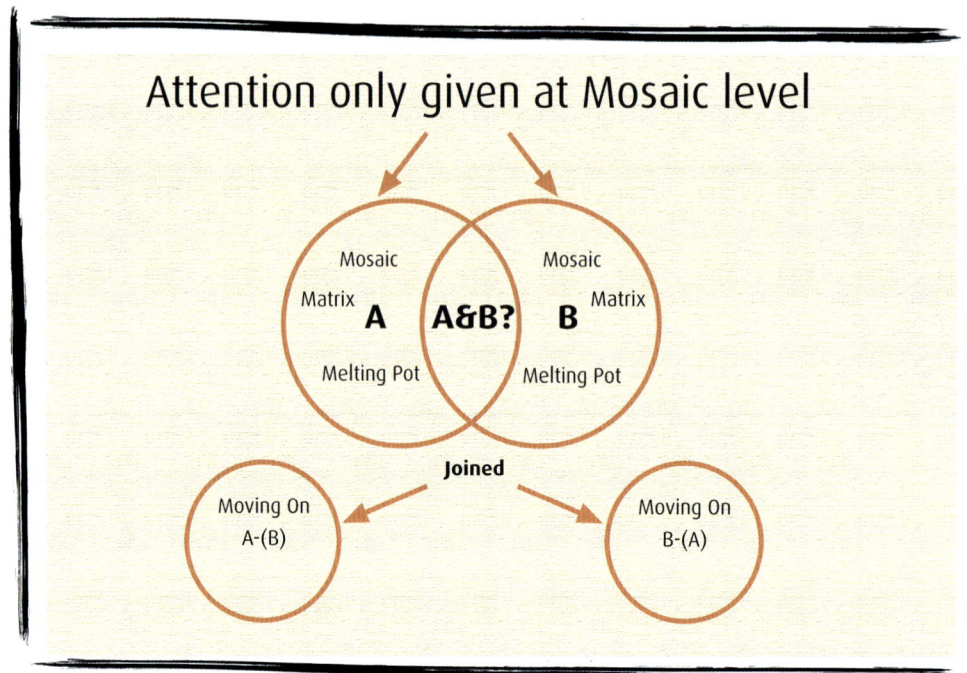

Attention only given at Mosaic level

Mosaic

Matrix

A   **A&B?**   **B**

Mosaic

Matrix

Melting Pot

Melting Pot

Joined

Moving On
A-(B)

Moving On
B-(A)

The negative cycle which becomes self-perpetuating where cultures have not been meshed at the 'Melting Pot' level leads to cultural breakdown. The warning signs are:

People in the merged organisation are not given an opportunity to be open about the organisation's cultures, its similarities and differences and about their feelings, hopes, fears, ambitions. At the melting pot level communication is stifled. Instead of common purpose being created to provide the new organisation with a common reference point, pre-joining instincts, rules and patterns of behaviour continue as before. No new joint legacy is created and no attempt to regenerate Identity, Significance, and Competence takes place.

Individuals and teams focus on non-productive similarities and differences. There is a heightened awareness and focus on actual and fictitious, non-productive relationships.

In an effort to ensure the deal goes through successfully management teams on both sides agree to everything in principle - and then fail to make the changes in practice by not engaging in melting pot activities.

Constituent teams and individuals start to exaggerate the swing back towards the cultural extremes embodied by their previous organisations.

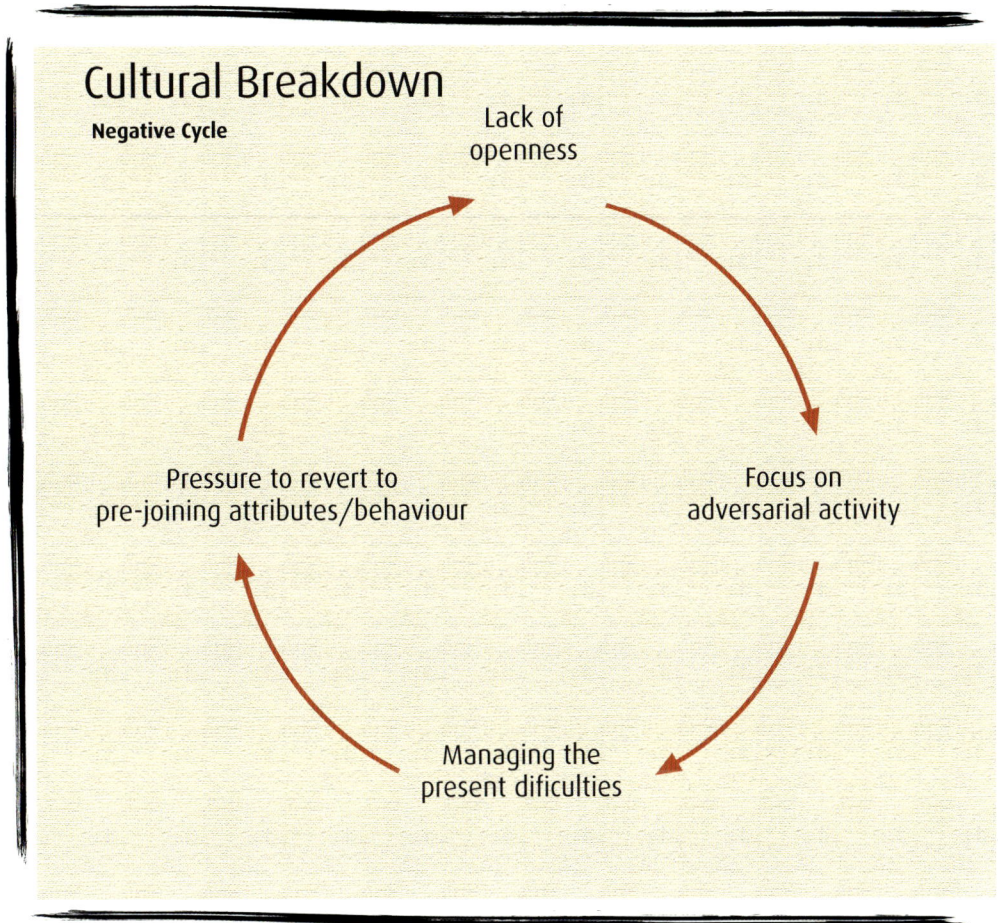

Cultural Breakdown
Negative Cycle

- Lack of openness
- Focus on adversarial activity
- Managing the present dificulties
- Pressure to revert to pre-joining attributes/behaviour

Creating a new hybrid

Where both organisations or, in a joint venture, all parties open up their boundaries, the joining phase becomes a regenerative point of acculturation where new foundations can be built on the strengths of the previous cultures. When acute attention is given to integrating cultures at Mosiac, Matrix and Melting Pot level and the hoped for one plus one equals infinity outcome is reached, then a new hybrid Is ready for its next opportunity for acculturation.

Creating a new Hybrid Culture

New Hybrid A+B+

A → ← B

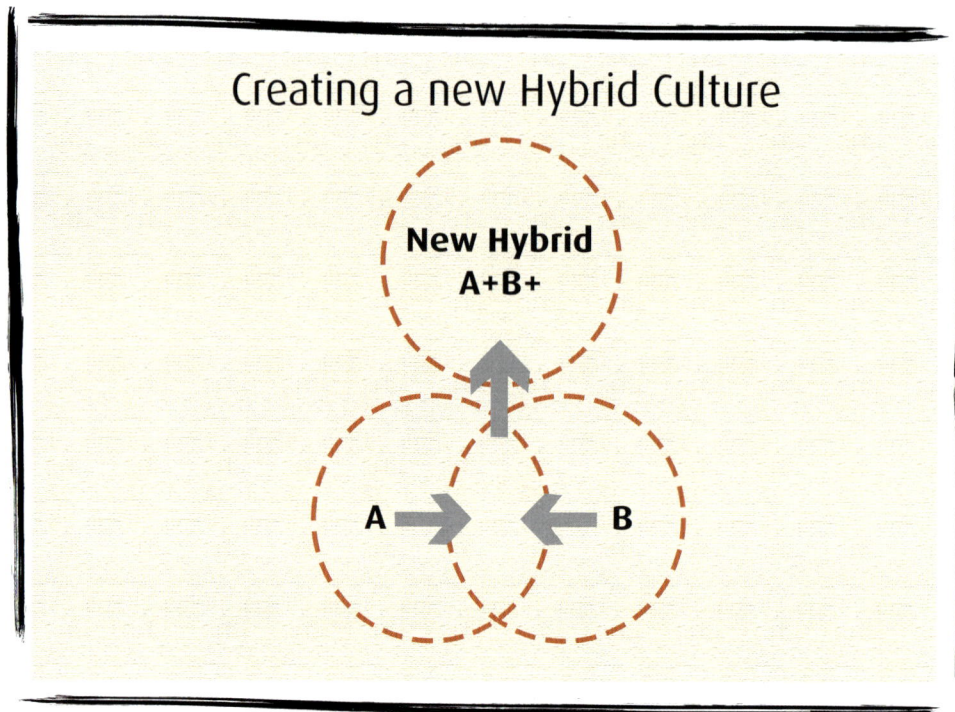

Properly led with cultures aligned and changed at a deep-structure level there is every likelihood of a successful outcome.

To ensure a successful cultural merger a number of steps have to take place:

Firstly, pre-joining an opening of the boundaries between the two organisations needs to take place so that mutual understanding is developed. This means, at the due-diligence stage, drilling down into your own culture and that of your prospective partner. This way a mutually rewarding understanding of cultural compatibilities and differences can be arrived at. The time and resources invested at this stage will pay dividends in creating the new hybrid.

Open Boundaries

Brand

Culture

Brand

Culture

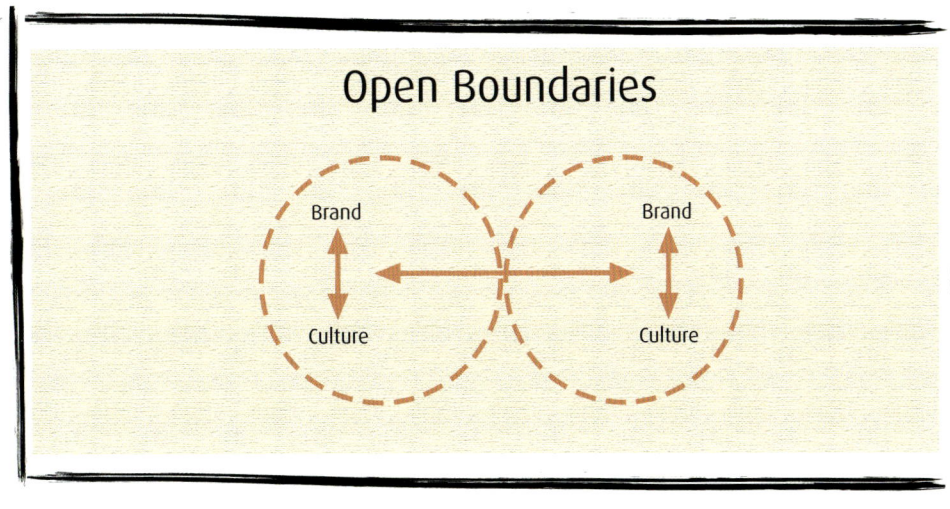

Immediately the joining process begins then expanding the interaction space between both organisations should be the principal focus for the new leadership team. However compatible at the mosaic and matrix level both cultures are founded on different experiences and focused on leaving different legacies, so understanding where there Is a fit or not is vital.

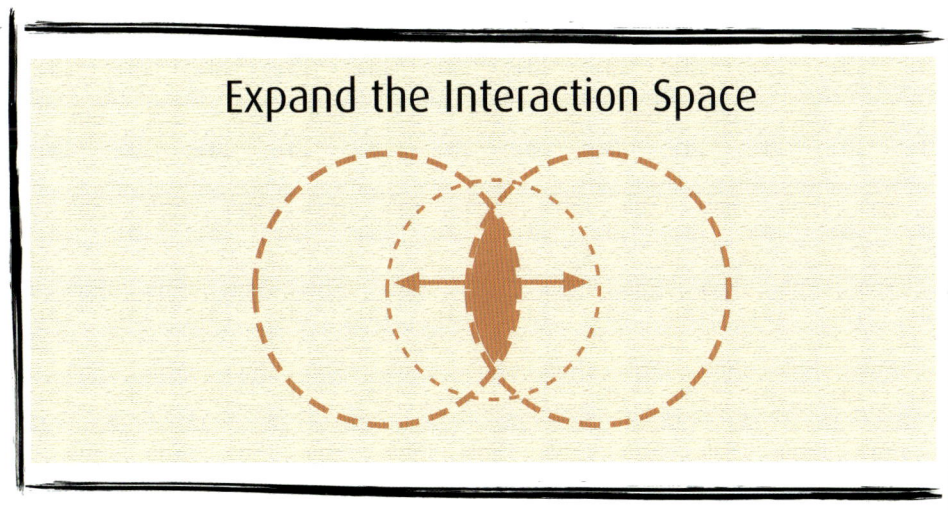

Expand the Interaction Space

Then, identify useful similarities and differences between the organisations as well as non-useful similarities and differences. A useful similarity might be that both organisations are strongly future-focused. A useful difference could be where one organisation is essentially cost reduction-focused and the other is predominantly innovation-focused. Then initiate regenerative activities to create the new entities, identity, significance, and competence.

This will ensure new, common purpose, common legacy and common organising capability. The significant stakeholders will have been involved in the re-generation so that the co-creation of the new entity has enabled the co creation of a new stakeholder constellation.

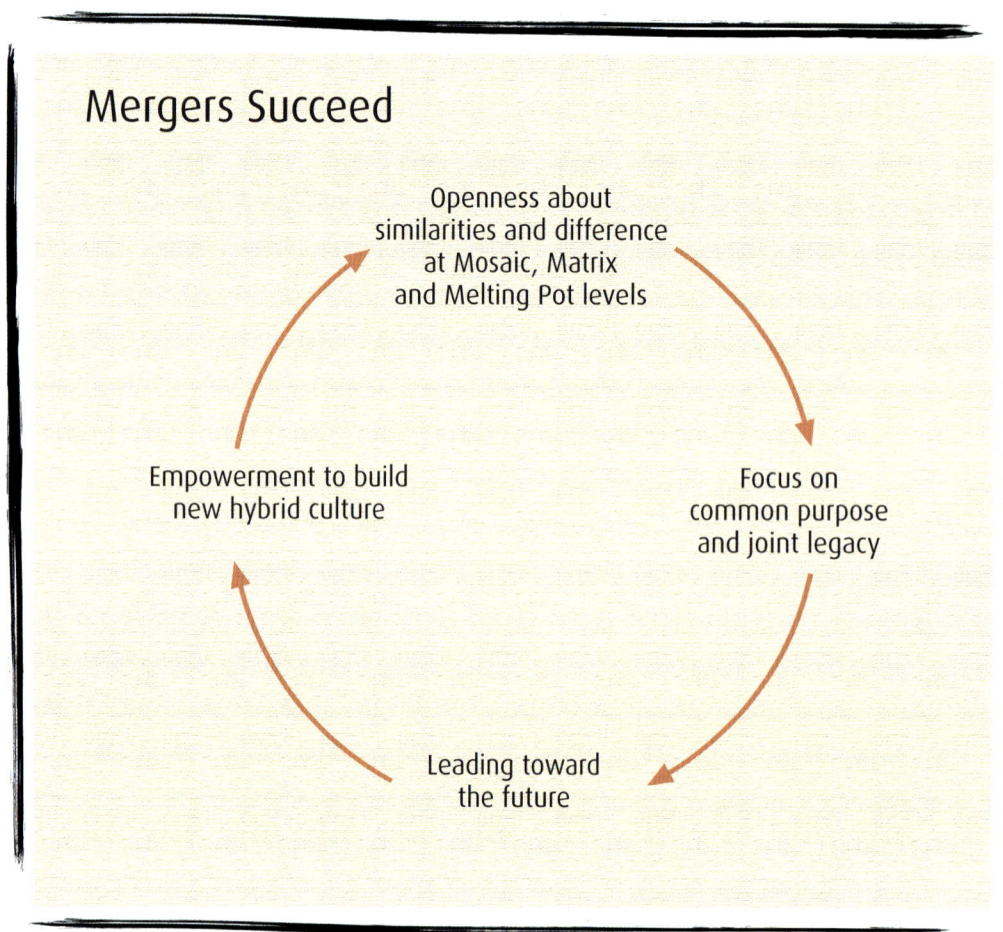

Mergers Succeed

Openness about
similarities and difference
at Mosaic, Matrix
and Melting Pot levels

Focus on
common purpose
and joint legacy

Leading toward
the future

Empowerment to build
new hybrid culture

In summary, the "due diligence phase" leading up to any proposed organisation combination typically concentrates on legal, financial, accounting and logistical issues as well as compatibility in markets and products and service offerings. These are, of course, all core components of any deal and their compatibility or 'fit' will provide the overarching rationale for taking the deal forward to completion. However, this early stage of the process is also the time leaders in both organisations should be taking the time to understand their own (if they haven't done so already) and their intended partner's deep-level cultural drivers. Understanding that there is an external fit between brands is one thing. So is taking a good look at matrix-level organisational structures and assessing their compatibility. But without a real understanding having been achieved at the deep-structure melting pot level there is less chance of the post-joining integration process progressing smoothly.

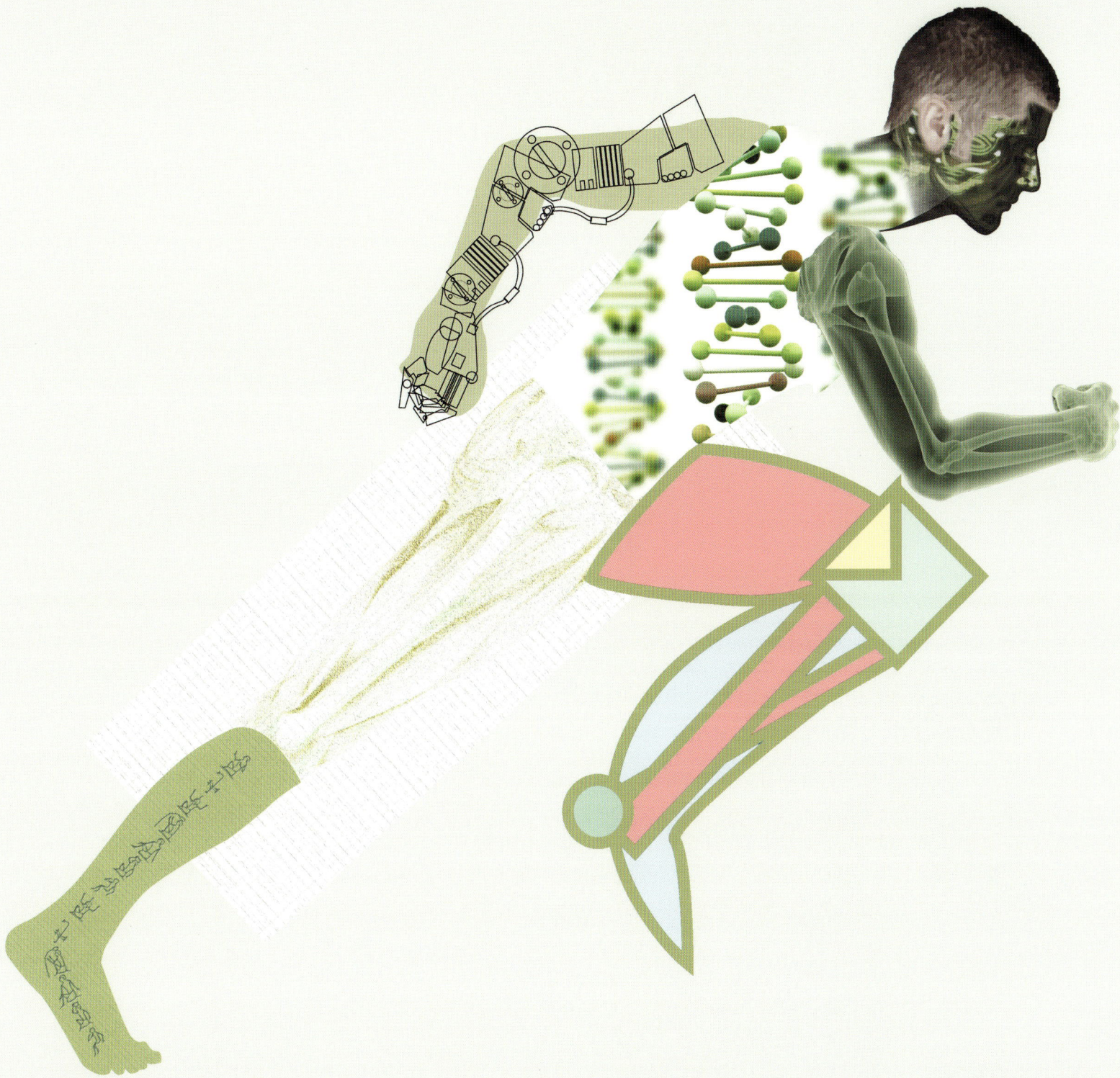

LEADING REGENERATION & CO-CREATION
Commercial, Social, and Ethical Intelligence

In regeneration leaders and teams need to start with themselves: Working through their own cycle of Identity, Significance, and Competence will enable them to engage and inspire their stakeholders towards their common legacy.

When organisations and individuals are degenerating, post mortems reveal 'moments of truth'. When, if the 'right things' had been said and done the downward spiral could have reverted to a regenerative defining point, where new more useful ethical intelligence could be forged.

Continued leadership appeasement of degeneration means the leaders' behaviours must be seen as irrational reactions at a reflex level. These reflex blocks can be seen as either deviant manifestations of overused strengths, fear based driven behaviour or negative beliefs that engage leaders in self defeating behaviour, these blocks need to be dealt with or mastered.

The individual leader, the teams they lead, the squads the teams are drawn from and the community of which they are all part need to resolve their Identity, Significance, and Competence so that they are nested within each other and aligned. This process will allow for stakeholder's needs and leadership aspirations to connect.

Being clear about who your stakeholders are and, are not, ensure they are given the appropriate differentiated attention so that their diverse needs are met in a co-creative process.

Rather than waiting for a crisis, governance agencies need to ensure that organisations are regularly resetting, recalibrating and abiding by their commercial, social, and ethical compass.

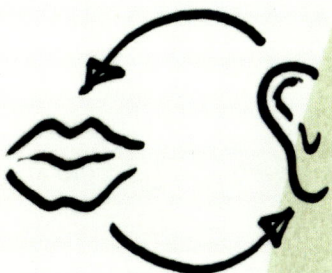

START WITH SELF

CO - CREATION

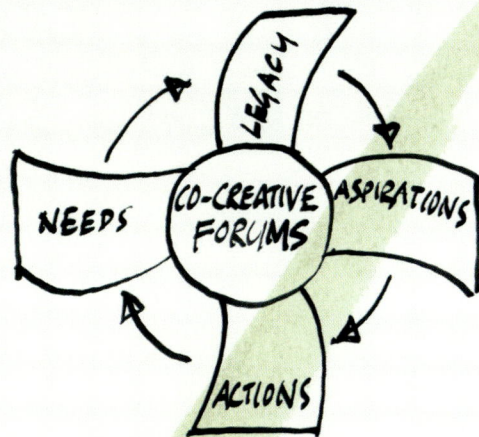

CO-CREATIVE FORUMS

LEGACY

NEEDS

ASPIRATIONS

ACTIONS

EFFECTIVE DOING REQUIRES AUTHENTIC BEING

CHARACTER

FORGED   FUDGED

POSITIVE BELIEF

ENHANCED RELATIONSHIP + ENABLING MINDSET

CO-CREATIVE BEHAVIOUR

POWER + CONTROL

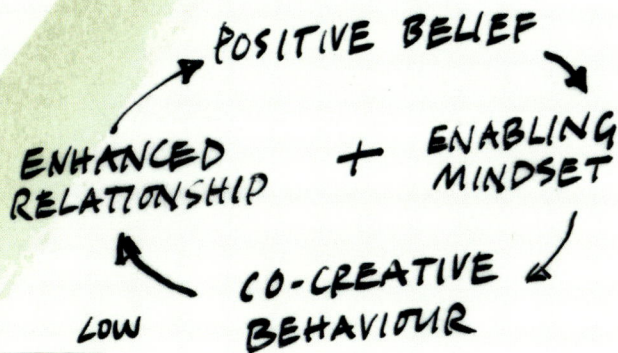

HIGH   LOW

POWER HELD OVER

POWER GIVEN TO

LOW   HIGH

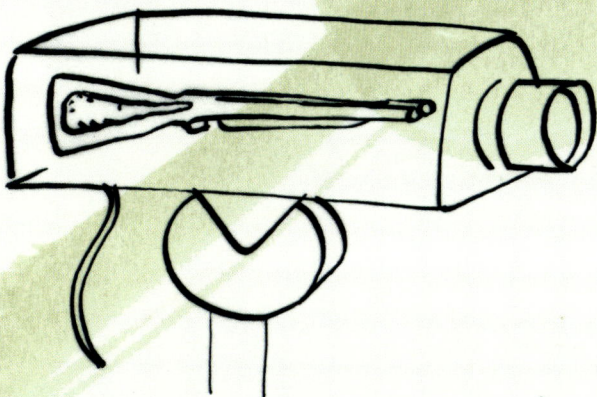

NEGATIVE BELIEF

ENTRENCHMENT OF PATTERN — DISABLING MINDSET

SELF DEFEATING BEHAVIOUR

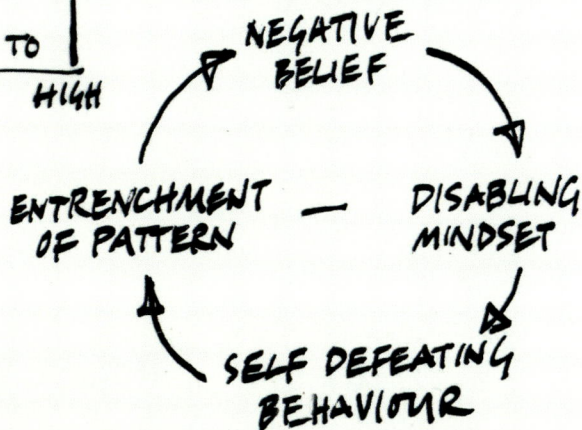

LEADING REGENERATION –
COMMERCIAL, SOCIAL AND ETHICAL INTELLIGENCE

Start with Yourself

Leadership Character -
Moments of Truth

Governance

The Stakeholder Universe

Sustainable Conversations

Forums for change

Start - Taking the Best Forward

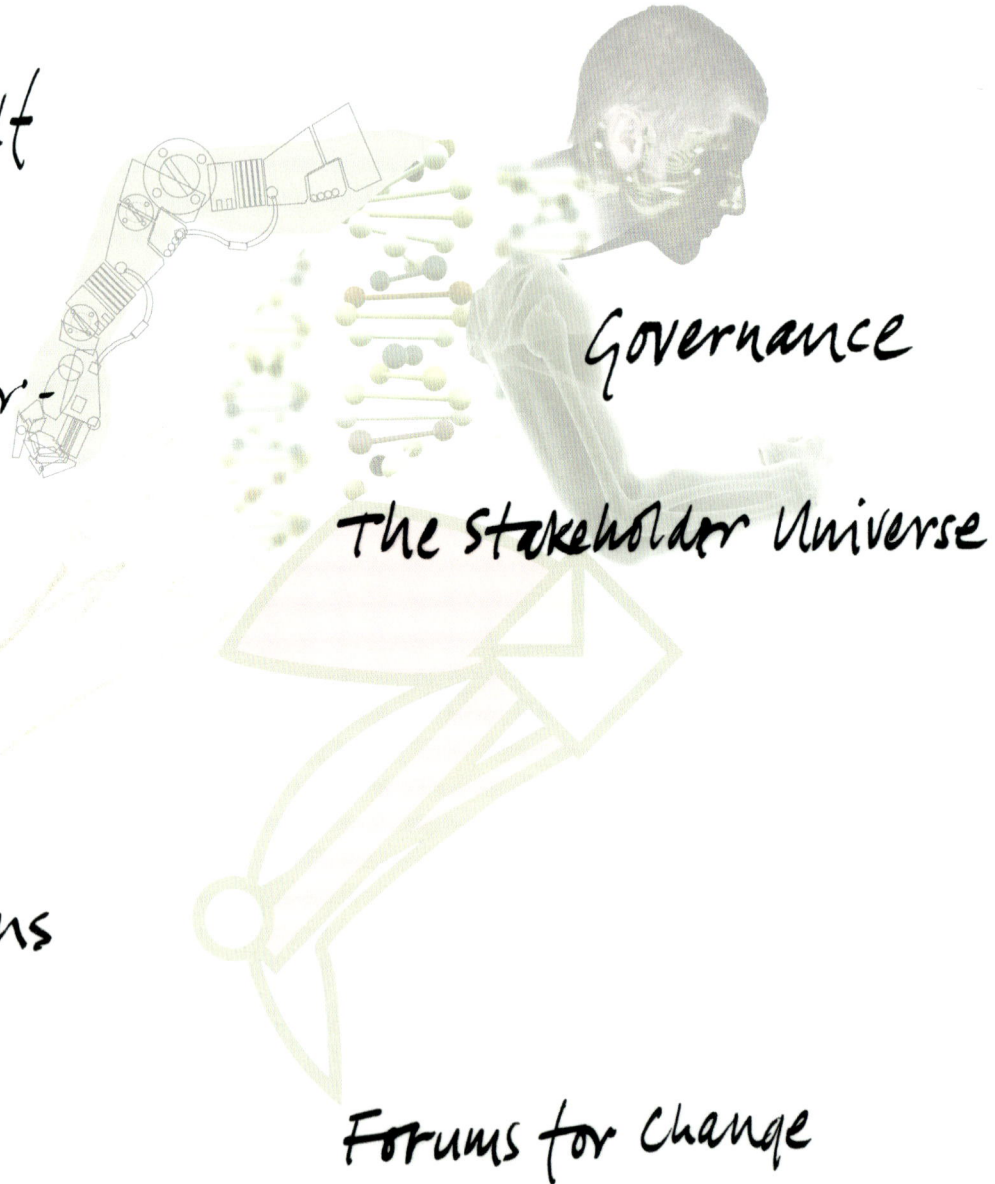

LEADING REGENERATION & CO-CREATION

The scope of the opportunities and challenges that face the Regenerative Leader are now clear. Their work is to embed regenerative and co-creative change cycles in their organisation and for their stakeholders that will sustain profitable growth over generations. This entails ensuring that the Identity, Significance and Competence of their organisation is always relevant, always slightly ahead of its time in meeting its stakeholders' needs.

- The organisation's Brand and Culture work as a virtuous cycle, one building on the other, with a clear line of sight between them ensuring that the shine within and the external dazzle have a cumulative effect.

- The Prophecy and Legacy complement and add to each other by bringing wise guidance to action that fundamentally enhances the life of the stakeholders.

- The Competence that the organisation expresses is fuelled by Identity and focused on Significance in a way that ensures that its organising capability is continually honed and enhanced.

- The necessary Stakeholder conversations take place to Co-create the added value needed by all significant parties.

- The Deep Structure Paradoxical Needs of all significant Stakeholders are understood and resolved in action that leads toward the legacy.

- The numerous Relationship Journeys they are responsible for are designed and undertaken so that all beginnings are optimal, all achievements are met and marked and moving on happens in an enabling, timely and graceful manner with due celebration.

- The Acculturation process is tended to at a Mosaic, Matrix and Melting Pot level so that crucial needs are met and the right judgements are made to ensure that the behaviour, the manifestation of culture is potent in the service of delivering the legacy, outcomes and outputs.

- The Continuity of Past, Present and Future is respected so that success is built on success and what clearly needs to change is changed. Seeing, understanding and transforming the tidal patterns at play in the deep structure of the organisation over the long term as well as meeting the demands of the present.

- The Commercial, Social and Ethical Compass of the organisation is in robust health and is used by all stakeholders to guide their actions.

So, an awfully complex list of jobs or a great adventure beckoning? It really does depend on the leader, their needs, instincts, values, and motivations: Are they earnest achievers, striving, shaping doing their best to get the right outcome or experts trying to prove that their tools and processes are the best at getting the job done. Or, masters of the strategic universe here to transform the world, save us and aggrandise themselves? All of these leadership mindsets can make a difference in small and spectacular ways but, the effects will always be short lived given that they are an expression of a leaders personality or stage of maturity rather than attempts to meet unfolding, deep rooted stakeholder needs. These mindsets or variants of them are often ones which young leaders bring to their 'early work' and can be a starting point from which their own regenerative leadership quest takes off. Leaders can only pretend to be perfect to be complete. In reality people are all 'works in progress' and the only choice they have is to take as much charge of their journey as they can or want to. Leaders who need to be always rooted in their present and future context have to continually regenerate their own Identity, Significance, and Competence. When the leader's and the organisation's regenerative journeys are aligned and synchronous then traction is applied and legacies can be achieved.

START WITH YOUR SELF

The individual's regenerative journey as a leader demands that they continually address and resolve the underlying paradoxes of Identity, Significance, and Competence.

Identity

The first paradox of identity addresses the need for leaders to change and remain the same.

Identity -   What do I need to change in myself to be the best leader I can become?
          -    What do I need to retain and tune to be the best leader I can become?

The paradox here is working at the elemental presence being level, rather than the doing level of competence. This paradox begs the initial question – "Do I need to change?" In all spheres of life where leadership can be taken and given; whether politics, sport, commerce, education; effective leaders need to continually rebase themselves; decide who they are now, what they want to achieve and the skills required to deliver in order to remain relevant. Stakeholders' needs are always changing so if leaders remain the same they are likely to be hounded out or ignored by constituencies that were once, not so long ago, lauding and applauding them.

So, once a leader comes to the conclusion that they will need to change, the next step is to decide what to change and what to retain and either amplify or tone down.

Leaders are all clumsy to varying degrees of effect, from slight distraction to huge destruction, so it is always possible to become less clumsy. Leaders need to be responsible for gathering personal feedback about themselves and what they need to change and retain from their significant stakeholders and, the stakeholders have the responsibility to ensure and insist that this feedback is given and attended to. Leaders are therefore not just on their own in determining what they need to do to develop and grow - and if they pretend they are - they will spend a lot of time experimenting on being different, stumbling around in the dark, crashing into their stakeholders' furniture rather than having a co-created navigable path toward joint success.

Becoming less clumsy and more elegant is a lifelong leadership quest, as is the search to be a distinctive voice in a strong affinity group. This means resolving the second paradox of Identity.

Identity   -   How to be a distinct enough leader to be exciting
              -       How to be a similar enough leader to connect

Leaders need to bring their own and their stakeholders' needs, judgments and behaviour to the context they want to work within. What personal brand do they need to exhibit to be different, interesting, attractive and compelling? What personal culture do they express to connect, to build trust, affection and loyalty? What do they need to be and do for others to love them enough to follow them?

Being and Doing

Key to this is the connection between being and doing. Identity is about who the leader is, how they define themselves and are defined by others, this is to do with elemental presence; with being. Doing is the manifestation of Being and is concerned with the expression of Competence. Competence should be fuelled by Identity but not confused with it.

Organisations conduct themselves in a manner that ensures there is always something to **do**. People are beset with a huge volume of noisy views, requests, demands for their time and attention. A great deal of this noise will represent the transient whims or the knee jerk reactions of an organisational population 'desperate to succeed' and 'scared to be seen to fail'. Leaders are then faced with individuals and teams who are extremely busy, urgently doing things/anything, which will range in nature from the nonsensical to mission critical. Ensuring that there is space and time for reflection for individuals and teams to understand the deeper purpose of who and what they need to be in order to usefully focus what they do is a mark of regenerative leadership.

Working from a 'being' mindset allows for a perspective that takes on the wholeness of relationships and situations; noticing patterns, trends and points of possible integration. 'Doing' necessarily focuses on segmenting relationships and situations into the next doable chunk. Therefore effective 'doing' requires authentic 'being'. For 'being' to be authentic it needs to be rooted in the ethical intelligence of regeneration, a sense of being responsible for the web or the fabric which underpins and pervades all attempts to communicate and influence not just single results but the manner in which relationships are created and conducted. Leaders are not just instruments of change but responsible for the manner in which the world changes.

A regenerative leader's identity displays the vulnerability, the playfulness, the curiosity, concern and love that go with **being** as well as the authority, drive, focus, rigour and respect needed for effective **doing**.

It is vital to take the co-creative pause; where the leaders Identity or being is examined at the deep structure paradox level so that any rebasing or revivifying can be done to ensure future relevance. This regeneration will ensure that the qualities of the Leader, what they need, what they believe, their values, motivations, principles, what they stand for and against build on all that is best in their past as well as the adjustments they need to make to be a leader in their present and forseeable future. This is both a journey of rediscovery and discovery.

Significance

The next level at which a leader has some choices about their future is Significance. How powerful do they want to be? What impact do they want to have?

The pairs of paradoxes that have to be resolved here are the need to succeed as a leader as well as have others succeed through their leadership and the need to make a fulfilling personal impact and to enable others to make the right impact on them.

These paradoxes talk to the need for the leader to reach some resolution on how they view and express power and control and how they view and use inclusion and exclusion. How these are resolved will determine how productive and fulfilled the leader and their stakeholders will be.

Leaders always approach their next regenerative opportunity with their own particular amalgam of elegance and clumsiness with regard to power and control and inclusiveness and exclusiveness strapped firmly to them. Un-packing this baggage and using their own sense and stakeholders' wisdom about what is needed to be accomplished, they then create their next blend of Prophecy and Legacy to propel and guide them forward through their next leadership adventure.

The first paradox that needs its particular contextual resolution is:

Significance -   How do I best succeed as a leader?
          -   How do I enable others' best success as a leader?

This has to do with power and control.

Power and Control

All leaders have a stance on who is responsible for ensuring success. Ranging from the **self-centred** conviction that the leader is solely able to shape destiny to the **other centred** certainty that people can only change themselves and the job of the leader is just to enable their success. Both of these approaches are ego centric because they insist that there is only one best way of accomplishment and that is their way. Master and Servant are both intractable positions.

Ideally the degree and shape of power and control exerted over others or given and taken by others should follow the function of the tasks that are needed for success. There is always a choice of style and where this style is exercised in a manner that is not optimally tied to the function of the task there will be less efficiency of effort and potential long term organisational harm. So, a leader 'supervising' a highly ambiguous complex change programme will quickly become dysfunctional and exhausted, in the same way a leader 'facilitating' a small number of people in a simple two or three step process is likely to be patronising and become frustrated. This leadership style flexibility is discussed further in the competence section.

Co-Creation

Co-Creation

Regenerative leadership is about giving up the master and servant positions and abandoning the imposition or enabling of preset change agendas. It is concerned with harnessing and aligning all energies available (directive and facilitative) to a point where insight and foresight are focused on co-creation with the consequential surge of committed action from all stakeholders. This requires the leader to give up the conventional power positions and allow the co-creation of new thought, new feeling and new behaviour. This is a process which allows the sum of the stakeholders' similar and different needs, insight and foresight to be brought to a decision point for transcendent action to naturally flow from the conversation. This is often seen when senior leaders meet in 'top to top' arenas and forums to converse from first principal on core deep structure issues of mutual interest. The purpose of the forum is clear but preset posturing is discouraged. The outputs and legacies co-created in these forums often lead to transformed relationships and actions which transcend their different organisations previously entrenched positions. No voice is inherently dominant. In this dialogue all stakeholders speak and listen with the intent of finding integrative ways forward that leapfrog over present differences and deliver a better future for all stakeholders. The key is to harness the collective power to create new meaning in the moment rather that to bash each other with preset positions and demands. Regenerative change demands and requires that all levels of stakeholders adopt 'top to top' co-creative mindsets by continually putting the fundamental needs on the table rather than the often contradictory adversarial wants and wishes that dominate a lot of stakeholder discussion. This ensures that the parties with a stake in each other's success focus on that success. Or in the next best case they quickly understand they are no longer stakeholders in each other's success. They may have become so engaged in niggling and fighting each other they failed to notice that they no longer have a jointly profitable common purpose. Time to move on.

So, co-creating the future means everyone's success building success. This leads to stable rooted prophecy based not just on guesses about the future but the collective wisdom building a wise guide for all stakeholders. The integrative sweet spot which ensures the paradox is resolved comes when meaning is made in the moment joint purpose is forged in live time, leaders are followers and followers are leaders. All engaged in co-creating a new pattern of possibility.

The second paradox moves us forward from success to fulfilment, getting it right is never enough, there is a deep need to make a lasting difference.

Significance -   How to make a lasting, fulfilling impact
            -    How to ensure others reach fulfilment

Inclusion and Exclusion

The impact we need to make and the impact we need from others to reach fulfilment are concerned with inclusion and exclusion. Leaders are always making choices about whom to include and whom to exclude in their prophecies about the future and the number and nature of the relationship they choose will determine the extent and longevity of their impact.

By choosing the relationships with which to have a mutually fulfilling impact leaders govern the scope and power of the difference they make. Choosing just to alleviate their local, present discomfort or attain easily reachable goals prompts leaders to choose shallower and closer sets of stakeholders. When a leader chooses to attempt to fundamentally transform the world in which they lead they will have to work at a deep level of relationship with a wide range of stakeholders who can influence greater numbers of constituencies to make the big differences that will have lasting generational effect.

The individual leader, their leadership teams and the stakeholder groupings have to choose the degree of significance they want to exert on their world to decide how powerful they want to be. Leaders can and do blinker themselves by focussing on leading the next phase of activity rather than starting with the end in mind; by constructing a sense of what they want to accomplish with their whole life, to foresee what, when they look back from old age will give them a sense of fulfilment. Having some clarity at whatever stage in life about what the ideal end game would be informs and propels our next immediate action. So, having a legacy in mind will inform our medium term visions and short term plans. Organisations however, are littered with leaders, many of whom will have been very extrinsically successful with all the trappings, the homes, the money and the yachts who will also be asking themselves "what was all that about?", "what impact did I make?", "was that all there was?", "how come I feel empty about what I've achieved?". They have no sense of leaving a bequest behind, of creating a legacy on which the next generation can build.

Once leaders decide to make a real difference it becomes clear that they can't do it on their own. Real impact comes from building a wide range of focused stakeholders with a deep commitment to each other's legacies. To invent the future you need you have to include and exclude judiciously. Too few shallow relationships mean limited aspirations and excluding no one will lead to diffuse, watered down legacies and action. Starting with the end in mind allows leaders to judge more clearly who they need to join and move on from in order to produce the fulfilment they require.

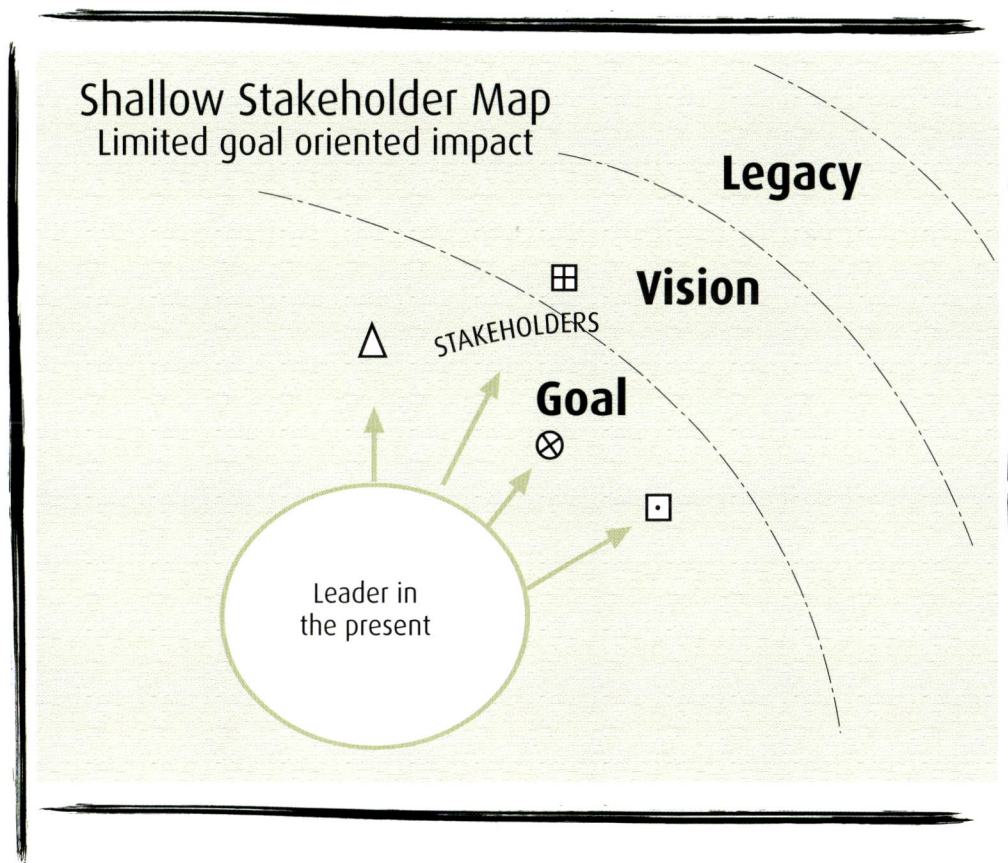

Shallow Stakeholder Map
Limited goal oriented impact

Legacy

Vision

STAKEHOLDERS

Goal

Leader in
the present

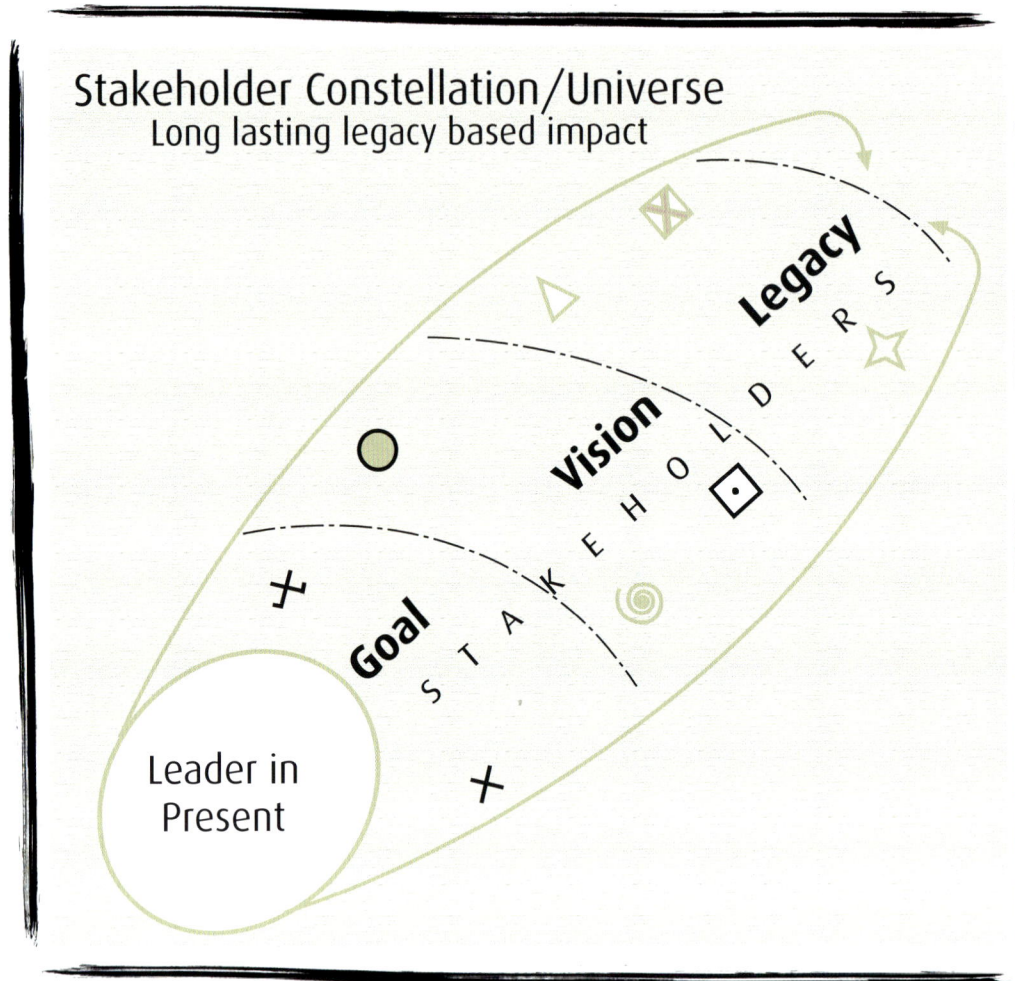

Stakeholder Constellation/Universe
Long lasting legacy based impact

Legacy

Vision

Goal

STAKEHOLDERS

Leader in Present

COMPETENCE

The first paradox of Competence is:

Competence -   Being in control of others
         -   Having others in control of me

How to be in control and have others in control continues the discussion started in the previous Significance section about the style choice a leader has in the way they ensure their own and others' productivity and therefore success. Having a wider range of style in the area of control, so that the form of leadership matches the function of the task to be performed, is a judgment issue at the Significance level, but it is also an action issue at the Competence level. Am I competent at using the leadership style I value flexibly?

Put simply, leaders potentially have power and control in a number of crucial areas of the system in which they operate. They can make choices about:

- Which stakeholders to engage with.

- The inputs they include or exclude to their organisation.

- Creating and maintaining the transformational value adding processes of their organisation.

- Creating and maintaining the feedback processes between their stakeholders.

- Creating and maintaining the quantity and quality of the outputs, outcomes, and legacies from the organisation.

Potentially, who is in control of making these choices ranges from power being exercised by those at the top of the organisation leading yet not actually engaged in the activity, to power being given to and taken by those involved in the task. To share power in this way is to move toward co-creation. Control needs to be devolved to the point where it will meet the need of the organisation to sustain and regenerate itself and its stakeholder relationships over time. The organising activities available to a leader can be matched against power in the following way. (See diagram overleaf)

Organising Activities

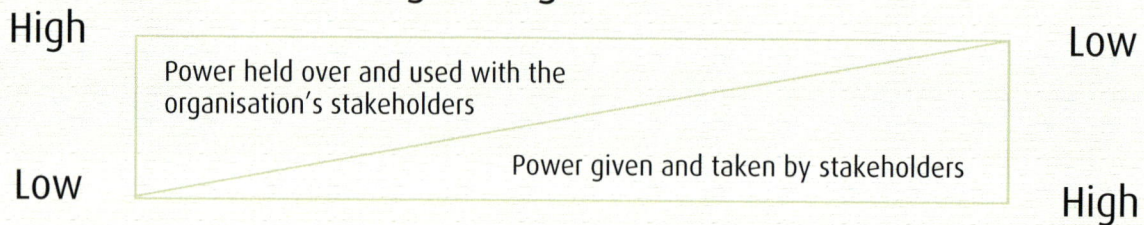

High   Low

Power held over and used with the
organisation's stakeholders

Power given and taken by stakeholders

Low   High

Leader as Supervisor	Leader as Manager	Leader as Visionary	Leader as Coach	Leader as Catalytic Facilitator
• Setting Tasks • Targeting • Monitoring • Evaluating • Disciplining • Rewarding	• Planning • Delegating • Motivating • Designing Process • Maintaining Process • Limiting Interference	• Providing Purpose and Meaning • Providing Long Term Prophecy • Evoking Individual and organisational excitement • Engage innovation and creativity	• Eliciting Performance Goals • Reviewing Progress • Extracting Learning • Planning Continuous improvement • Create a learning environment	• Enabling others to learn how to learn • Sponsoring and enabling co-creation • Promoting both being and doing • Generating Legacy • Promoting regeneration • Encouraging experimentation and risk taking

All of these types of leadership are valid and vital for an organisation's success. The goal of the regenerative leader is to be usefully flexible in using all of these leadership 'muscles' and to exercise them appropriately depending on the work they are engaged in and the attendant relationships they are trying to create.

There is also a historical continuum of the focus of organising activity with regard to power. When the manufacture of goods and the provision of services was a fairly straightforward set of processes in a slowly changing world, where the differentiation of what was offered was relatively simple, it was possible to have an organising focus mostly consisting of management and supervision. As goods and services have become instantly replicable by competitors; people's aspirations about the quality of their contribution and their life have increased; and change in a turbulent world has become the only stable state - some form of empowerment and therefore the need for a focus on organising activities such as visioning, coaching and catalytic facilitation which foster empowerment have become essential. Another major indicator of the need for the activities which allow potential empowerment is that stakeholders have become more discerning and demanding. The moan that 'stakeholders are becoming more assertive' is heard at all levels in organisations. The appropriate response is to empower those at the boundary with the stakeholder to satisfy and resolve the issue or opportunity at first contact or to recover and positively transform the relationship after a breakdown.

Strangely, as Leaders have become more aware of the turbulence that is endemic in their ever changing world, many have felt a need to become more controlling rather than more empowering. Pressure results in the leader moving to their 'default position' use of power. There is value in keeping task definition, standard procedures and costs 'tight', but also to allow for 'loose' forms of response, therefore, making sure that the discretion to get things done sits where it is useful, at the boundary with the stakeholder, rather than where it sits most comfortably, usually at the top of a hierarchy. This ability to exercise 'tight' and 'loose' control at the same time is critical for organisations to flourish.

Catalytic facilitation and Coaching are distinct from the other forms of organising activity in that their primary intent is to enable others to become more competent, efficient, creative and powerful. These states may be an outcome of good visioning, management and supervision but is not their primary intent. This is not to say that Catalytic facilitation and Coaching are not concerned with more effective task completion, they are. But they are also concerned with the more effective completion of the next task and the task after that, as well as the continuing relationship journey of the people whose job it is to make the difference. Rather than remaining dependent on the ongoing energy of a supervisor, manager or visionary they learn how to regenerate their own.

Running parallel to the ideas of empowerment through coaching and Catalytic facilitation is the movement away from individual responsibility, action and reward toward stakeholder responsibility, action and reward; toward co-creation. Team working is where facilitation and co-creation as an organising focus really comes into its own. When the group moves from being led to being facilitated by its leader or to being facilitated by the person most appropriate to the circumstances that the team is meeting in, then it is possible to flatten hierarchies, build useful long-term relationships with stakeholders, and release more creativity into the organisation. Using catalytic facilitation, people feel more able to personally contribute to problem solving, error reduction and the generation of novel processes and solutions. This will engage everyone in their part of the deeper regeneration process, thereby, helping organisations move toward productivity and fulfilment.

The regenerative leader therefore, has the responsibility to ensure that Competence is expressed, so that the form of control matches the function of the outputs, outcomes, and legacies needed. This requires the flexible use of the leader's and follower's control muscles in the service of meeting stakeholder needs.

What is needed in terms of focus of organising activity, for form to follow function, will depend on whether a number of optimal conditions are met or not met.

These include:

Supervision

- The work is new/novel to the person doing it.
- The work can be observed by the supervisor.
- The required outputs are reasonably predictable and uniform.
- The number of people interactions needed to get the work done are minimal.
- The tasks are concrete and measurable, rather than ambiguous.
- Compliance is really all that is needed to ensure some success.
- There is some legal or ethical need to assess competence and integrity for the wider good.

Management

- Work can only be successfully completed through others' efforts.
- A set of tactics is needed to move from inputs to outputs.
- Work can be done in more than one way.
- People need to understand and accept a common set of objectives.
- People need to be motivated to perform well in their work.
- There is a high reliance on information systems, processes, and procedures.
- There needs to be individual responsibility for costs, revenue and profit.
- Tasks exist within agreed and measurable parameters.

Visioning/Coaching

- A strategy aligning organisational effort with the stakeholder need is necessary.
- It is not possible to be aware of everything that is being done in the system.
- A shared vision of the future is essential to organisation success.
- A clear understanding of what the system exists to do, its identity will bind people together and focus them on their stakeholders needs.
- A high degree of commitment to the organisations significance is necessary for success.
- Tasks are ambiguous, changeable and hard to measure.

Catalytic Facilitation

- A legacy connecting the organisation to the long term satisfaction of stakeholder needs is necessary.
- Shortening learning times, is necessary to meet complex demands and changes in the stakeholder's needs.
- Innovation and Co-creation are necessary for long-term success.
- Long chains of command are seen as detrimental.
- People demand to be fully involved in most aspects of what they do.
- The nature of the stakeholder relationship journey is as important as the product or service.

In the Regeneration process all the organising activities of the leader will be necessary, however, the activity needs to be underpinned and fuelled by a facilitative, catalytic mindset.

Competence -   How others learn from me
             -   How I learn from others

The other paradox of competence. Having others learn from you as well as learning from others is resolved usefully in the same way. Leadership and Followership are in a relational dance, they are intertwined; you can't lead without having followers and you can't follow without having leaders each are necessary and responsible for achievement and for learning. As well as being flexible in appropriately utilising the full range of organising activities, as leaders, they have to be open to engaging in the full range as a follower. Being open to and insisting on being appropriately supervised, managed, engaged, inspired, coached and facilitated not just as a hierarchy might dictate but by those who are best suited to the context, ensures the creation of a virtuous learning cycle where all leaders are followers and all followers leaders and everyone is appropriately responsible for learning.

SUSTAINABLE CONVERSATIONS

The regenerative leader's competence must, therefore, be mustered toward three connected and overlapping conversations. The common aim of these conversations is to engage and inspire individuals and teams to build a sustainable future for their stakeholders and enable their people to feel that they contribute meaningfully to a larger agenda not just the piece of work which is their direct daily responsibility. This creates emotional capital and promotes value based acculturation process. The three conversations are, for relationship, for accomplishment and for ongoing personal and professional development.

Conversations for Relationship

Productive leadership and followership is most realizable when people feel connected to their wider community, their organisation and the colleagues and the teams they work with, where there is a mutually appropriate sense of business intimacy. The conversation needs to be at three levels.

The Mosaic Level

The leader's work here is to be the catalyst to prompt and coach people within the organisation to have appropriate contact and connection with their stakeholders outside the organisation and to do so in such a way that the organisation's Brand equity is enhanced in the wider community. These connections, where the individual is a representative or ambassador for the organisation can be as diverse as being a community school governor, an office holder on a related professional body, attending or hosting social functions designed to build trusted customer or supplier relationships, joint working parties concerned with industry standards or benchmarking or business development activities.

The Matrix Level

In these conversations the individuals and teams need to connect appropriately to ensure that the internal dynamics of their organisations are aligned across their internal boundaries to produce the agreed outcomes and legacy and to deepen the relationships involved so that the next contact will always be richer and more profitable. Examples of the activities here would be; inter-divisional problem solving meetings, functions and operations representatives meeting in innovation forums, R & D and Marketing having joint visioning sessions. Here the leader's role is to engage, inspire, coach and facilitate their people to approach their internal relationships from an interdependent mindset so that everyone feels responsible, not just for the success of their own piece, but for ongoing success of each other and the whole enterprise.

The Melting Pot Level

Leaders need to ensure that their people engage and connect to the appropriate level with those who they have day to day contact and with whom they need to interact with in order to make their own personal difference. At this granular level there needs to be robust relationships where there is a great deal of knowledge about each other, a deep background to relate to. These colleagues need to know each other's instincts, values, likely behaviour, actions and reactions, hopes and fears. This level of intimacy is necessary to both build a raft to sustain the inevitable breakdowns and differences as well as maximise creativity. The leader and the follower have joint responsibility for provoking and evoking the melting pot, crucible like discussions that are necessary for regeneration to take place.

Forums for change here will be meetings such as those that facilitate feedback between team members ensuring that one to one conflict resolution occurs and formal team building and semi social events occur. Regenerative leaders and followers work with diversity to help people connect up their similarities and differences to ensure innovative sustainable achievements.

Business intimacy, where individuals and groups know and are known as social beings rather than just units of work that do tasks, is essential if the many relationship journeys they are engaged with are expected to flourish. Joining at a deeper human level, achieving a fulfilling outcome together and moving on with some regret at losing a personal connection are not just "nice to haves", they are prerequisites for organisational success.

Conversations for Accomplishment

The purpose here is to supervise, manage, coach and facilitate individuals and teams by agreeing appropriate processes to assure achievements. This needs to be done at three levels.

Legacy

How individuals and teams will fundamentally transform the landscape of what is presently done in order to deliver future generational value to stakeholders. Although this can be navigated by the leader and the team it will need engagement with the stakeholders to ensure the right needs are met to the right level.

Outcomes

What needs to be done to meet and exceed stakeholders' current expectations both qualitatively and quantitatively? To ensure that the short to medium term business planning process is delivering what it set out to accomplish.

Outputs

Ensuring that the day to day, month to month, quarter to quarter increases and decreases in areas such as turnover, profitability, costs, staff retention are on or better than budget. To ensure the operational promise is delivered.

Conversations for Development

Here the leadership/followership dance is concerned with ensuring that individuals and teams are equipped with the required personal, social and professional skills to succeed and grow in their work and their life. This is not just about helping them understand their strengths and building their capacity to capitalise on them or understanding their capability gaps and how to bridge them. It is also about conversations that enable greater confidence and emotional resilience and increase enjoyment and help maintain and build high levels of motivation and passion.

LEADERSHIP CHARACTER – MOMENTS OF TRUTH

When everything is working well Leadership is relatively easy. When people more or less know why they are there, what they need to do to succeed and are generally motivated and have some sense of fulfilment, all the leader needs to do, and even this is a lot to ask, to align their separate energies, to focus on creating outcomes and legacies that are more than the sum of their individual efforts. This will be possible because there is clear congruence between the individuals and the organisation's Identity and Significance and, therefore, everyone can contribute toward the edge of their best Competence.

Where the leader's own and/or their organisation's Identity, Significance, and Competence are being ignored, badly accommodated or challenged in an exploitative manner, either through acts of commission or omission, then the organisations will begin to become stuck and start to move toward the Degenerative spiral of Anomie, Notoriety and Mediocrity. Post mortems of these times when individuals and organisations start to slide backwards and begin to loose their compass always reveal moments of truth, when if the 'right things' had been said and done early then there would have been the possibility of a much more powerful positive outcome. These 'right things' , the right conversations relate to Identity, Significance and Competence and relate to leader's responsibility to unequivocally say "No" or "Yes", or "I don't believe you" in the defining moment.

Identity

A customer asks for special personal payment arrangements to facilitate/lubricate the smooth completion of a deal and this is accommodated.
A team member discloses propriety data to a competitor and this is ignored.
A leader verbally attacks a colleague's integrity in public and this is accepted.
A regulator is tardy or discriminates in the enforcement of its rules and is not held accountable for this.

Significance

A division continually has plausible explanations for its underperformance and these excuses are accepted.

An organisation accounts for its financial achievements in a manner which boosts executive bonuses and diminishes shareholder returns and this is ignored.

Divisional Managing Directors work against each other to maximise their individual division's success and minimise their colleague's success and no one confronts this negative pattern.

Leaders inspire their people and their shareholders with extraordinary visions of the future which can never happen and no one pricks their bubble.

Competence

Substandard service is provided to stakeholders and no one involved owns up to their part of the failure to deliver their operational promise.

A Chairman suspects his Executive Board is not following a relevant robust strategic planning process yet fails to bring his disquiet to them.

A peer knows one of his colleagues is continually not delivering to their agreed targets and feels this is none of their business and therefore doesn't interfere.

Serious lapses in health and safety procedure are detected by managers who cover up the faults.

In cases such as these, that happen everyday in organisations, it is the moments of truth when something could and should have been said and done that are the defining moments when leadership character is either forged or fudged. Most people in organisations, but particularly those who have chosen to accept designated leadership roles, tend to have an optimistic ideal that their instincts, values and principles will always play through into their behaviour. Most leaders believe they do and will tell the truth, support their colleagues, confront dysfunctional behaviour and work toward goals which are for the greater good of all their significant stakeholders. Yet, organisations are rife with semi true accommodations, overriding personal agendas, tacit and overt support for nonsensical behaviour and favouritism. These degenerations are inevitable and need to be minimised. However, these 'strange accumulations' do make regeneration an imperative because Regeneration means facing up to and dusting off the debris from times when moments of truth weren't grasped or capitalised on. They offer new beginnings based on the positive of the past. A chance to slough off the dead skin and start again.

There are a number of reasons why Moments of Truth aren't grasped and positively used as catalysts to build the social and ethical capital and intelligence of the leader and of the organisation's culture.

The simplest reason is that these moments when first encountered are unexpected, so leaders are not prepared to grasp the nettle as it rears up, they cough, shuffle and feel embarrassed, hoping what has happened or has been said didn't occur or will go away. If the moment is not grasped it is much harder to recover the high ground. Also, generally, leaders tend to think that their stakeholders are 'honourable people' just like them and can be shocked into inactivity by sudden unexpected exploitative behaviour.

At this level, planning, rehearsing and scripting of appropriate responses to exploitative 'alien invasions' is beneficial. Leaders and their teams need to think through potential breakdown points. To plan for likely moments of truth pertaining to each of their stakeholder's groups including their competition and prepare considered responses to any invitation to water down or betray their espoused values and principles.

Having clear responses which have the prior commitment of the board or the team - not just the conviction of the individual leader - and can be delivered with unequivocal assertion will move these moments of truth from the edge of a slippery slope to being the defining moment of a culture with increased ethical, social, and commercial intelligence.

When there is continuing appeasement of exploitative action then the disconnect between the leadership values/principles and their behaviours must be seen as irrational reactions at a reflex level, it is as if the leaders behaviour is not under their conscious control, they cant seem to stop themselves form colluding with something they know is not 'right' in relation to their espoused instincts, beliefs, values and principles. They are blocked in the moment and over time from being the best leader they can be.

BLOCKS TO REGENERATIVE LEADERSHIP

Blocks can be seen in loose categories which overlap and intertwine with each other:

- Deviant manifestations of overused strengths.

- Fear based driven behaviour.

- Negative beliefs that engage Leaders in self defeating behaviour.

Overused Strengths

Leaders, generally, bring their best intentions and skills to their organisational endeavours. They are conscious of their responsibilities and opportunities and know that they have to stretch themselves in order to accomplish what their stakeholders need from them. This stretch can often contain the seeds of a leaders vulnerability. It seems natural that stretch should mean that a leader does more of what they already do well now, to amplify their strength to a new pitch of intensity.

Often, unfortunately, this leads to overuse of a strength, tipping useful purposeful behaviour into self defeating and driven action with the consequent, negative outcomes for the organisation and its regenerative agenda.

It is precisely at the moment when a strength is needed that it can be overused in volume and intensity. These will be moments when the consequences of continued exploitation, inertia or failure will be at their highest and the resultant pressure or stress will be more likely to effect the judgement of the leader and therefore the manner in which they influence. In this way the wonderful gift of plain speaking can tip over into cruelty or bullying, the enabling capacity to collaborate can turn to semi cringing appeasement, the purposeful driving force of passion can become a frenzy of contradictory energy and effort, the care that is needed for stakeholders to flourish morphs into collusion with illegitimate needs and wants and the charisma necessary to generate organisational excitement becomes annoying insubstantial froth.

These negative tipping points are extremely confronting to the persona of the leader, confusing to their followership and are the makings of a great feast for the organisations cynics just waiting for the " I told you so, I knew she/he couldn't be that good" moment.

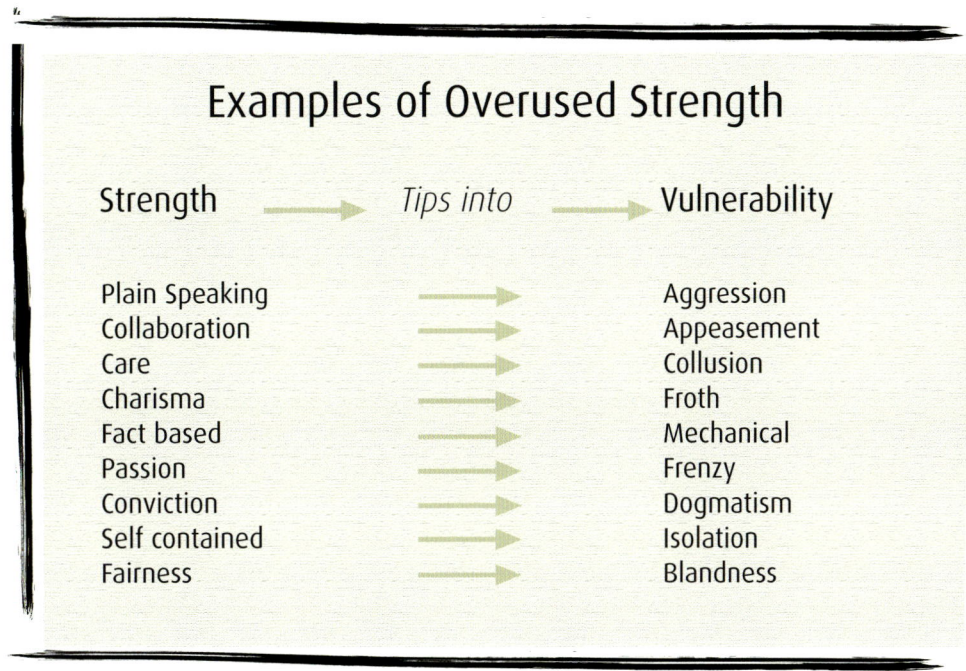

Examples of Overused Strength

Strength	Tips into	Vulnerability
Plain Speaking	→	Aggression
Collaboration	→	Appeasement
Care	→	Collusion
Charisma	→	Froth
Fact based	→	Mechanical
Passion	→	Frenzy
Conviction	→	Dogmatism
Self contained	→	Isolation
Fairness	→	Blandness

The underpinning mindset that ensures the continued existence of the tipping point from strength to overused strength is that people view the opposite of their strength as a weakness rather than the obverse of their strength as another complementary strength. So the choice is seen to be between good or bad, useful or non useful behaviour rather than the opportunity to find the most influential integrative point between two complementary strengths that absolutely fit the context they are presently in.

So, in endeavouring to maximise their strength a plain speaker is trying their best not to lie or be wishy washy, someone who cares is trying desperately not to be destructive or dismissive and a leader who prides themselves on being charismatic is straining every sinew to not be boring and dull.

Imagined Negative Opposites of Strength

Moving Away from	toward	Strength
Lying	→	Plain Speaking
Fighting	→	Collaboration
Uncontrolled	→	Self Contained
Lifeless	→	Passionate
Discriminatory	→	Fair
Unfeeling	→	Care

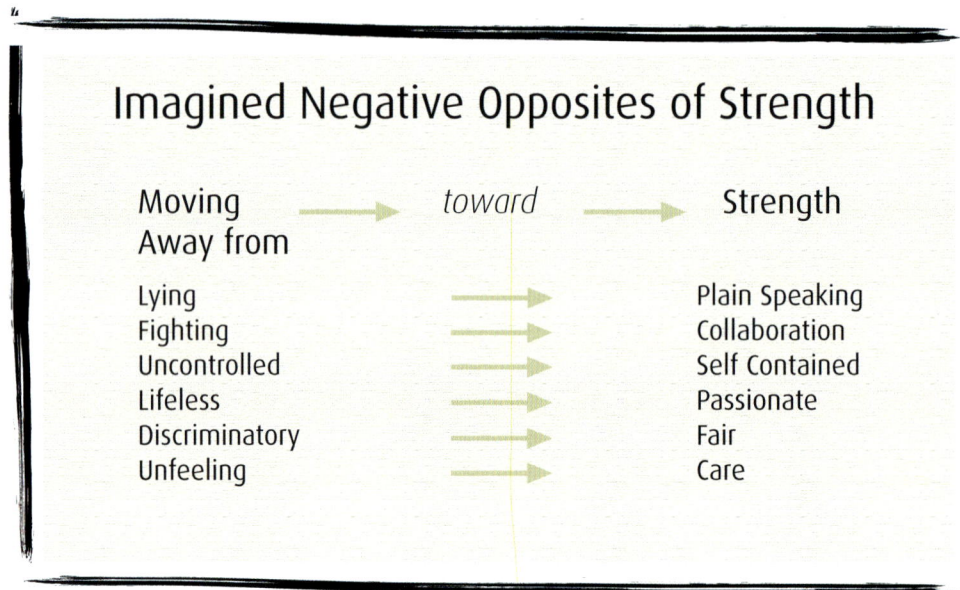

In moving away from what the leader has framed as being 'bad' toward their cherished strengths it leads to the potential of a double negative payoff in the moment of truth when behaviour is chosen. The thought is that "I must amplify my strength or I will appear weak". Therefore, the mindset that I must collaborate or I will end up fighting leads to appeasement. The conviction that I need to be self contained under pressure or I will loose all control ensures I end up isolated. The need to express the value of care in behaviour or I will be or be seen to be unfeeling is such an awful thought that I prefer to overuse my strength and collude in a 'caring' way with someone's self destructive or exploitative needs and actions.

Another option is to frame strength as a seemingly contradictory paradox which will be resolved in its most contextually useful way in the defining moment. In this way a guidance system is brought to the choice of which behaviour will be most appropriate.

The obverse of fairness is merit, competition is the necessary yin to the essential yang of collaboration. Directness is the catalytic twin that ensures care never becomes soppy and sentimental. Both poles of the paradox are now desirable goals and the issue becomes how the paradox is used to find the sweet spot

Examples of Paradoxical Choice

Overused	Strength	Integrated Strength
Aggression	Plain Speaking	Sensitive Directness
Appeasement	Collaboration	Joint Responsibility
Collusion	Care	Ruthless Compassion
Froth	Charisma	Pragmatic Excitement
Mechanical	Fact based	Provable Intuition
Frenzy	Passion	Purposeful Inspiration
Dogmatism	Conviction	Curious Certainty
Isolation	Self contained	Interdependent
Blandness	Fairness	Primus Inter Pares

amalgam of the best of both that suits the moment of truth currently in play.

For someone to recalibrate their strengths means they are adjusting, regenerating their sense of self; their identity. This will mean examining their reflex instincts, their seemingly natural uncontrolled reactions, when under pressure in stressful situations. This can be daunting as it is about unknitting what is in one sense a very useful and comfortable garment: their strengths. However, as long as a leader chooses to engage with others in worthwhile endeavour they will meet defining moments. These are choice points when they can either regenerate their moral, social and commercial capital or not. These moments of opportunity follow leaders around, they can't be escaped, so embracing them as useful paradoxical puzzles is the way forward.

Blocks as fear based driven behaviour

At the root of a leader's personal identity is a needs based guidance system that when working at its best leads them toward satisfying their needs and away from the negative consequences of not meeting their needs. Some of these negative consequences will be emotional and moving away from these emotions can become a need in its own right.

So rather than just fearing the negative emotion that will occur when a need is not met, the fear of the negative emotion becomes a motivator; whether a need is there or not. So, for example, the motivation moves from eating in order to gain sustainable nourishment to eating because we are fearful about being hungry. This is, of course, more likely to lead to overeating.

These concerns, fears and disabling worries come from early breakdowns in our personal and social development where our needs to have a fulfilling enough Identity, Significance, and Competence have not been fully satisfied. This leads to seemingly irrational fears which, as the pattern unfolds guarantee we end up in the condition our mindset and behaviour is trying to protect us from.

Realistic fears and concerns are absolutely essential to keep us safe as we move forward, however, if the fears start to engage self defeating behaviour they need examination and action.

A fear of failure can lead us to achieve but if unchecked can lead to setting only incremental goals which never really satisfy, a concern over intimacy can lead to distinct individuals or real loneliness, a questioning stance on how authority is used can lead to healthy interdependence or truculent rebellion. The tipping point will again occur in situations; defining moments, when the stress perceived moves the behaviour from a choice point of rational concern over reaching a goal, to a real fear that makes us move clumsily away from an imagined, amplified, emotional threat. Again there is the possibility of a double negative here as it is not just the fear of being foolish, for example, but the fear of being seen to be foolish that is the trigger. The consequent negative judgement we expect from others that flows from being caught in the act adds a layer of shame.

Fear Based Blocks

Fear of	_drives a_	Positive Outcome	_but can also lead to_	Negative Outcome
Failure		Success		Unsatisfying Goals
Being Foolish		Respect		Loss of Dignity
Intimacy		Rugged Individualism		Lonliness
Authority Figures		Interdependence		Co or Counter Dependence
Rejection		Acceptence		Isolation
Conflict		Harmony		Disconnection
Ambiguity		Clarity		Confusion

Blocks as Negative Belief Cycles

A further way of understanding how leaders block themselves from being the best leader they can become is that they sometimes choose not to examine the negative beliefs they hold about themselves and the consequences of their behaviour which click into place when they feel under stress. These negative beliefs, consequent mind sets and resultant self defeating behaviours are individualised and each leader will have their own distinct pattern of stopping themselves getting what they need and want.

So, one leader might have the negative belief that; if they express excitement people wont take them seriously, this will lead to a mindset of emotional cautiousness, which will lead to the stilted, flat presentation of an organisational vision which no one therefore takes seriously. Another leader may have a negative belief that; if they are serious other people wont enjoy being with them, this, under stress, leads to a mind set of convivial banter which leads to seemingly frivolous attention to important matters and in consequence others move away from them.

The Generalised Negative Cycle

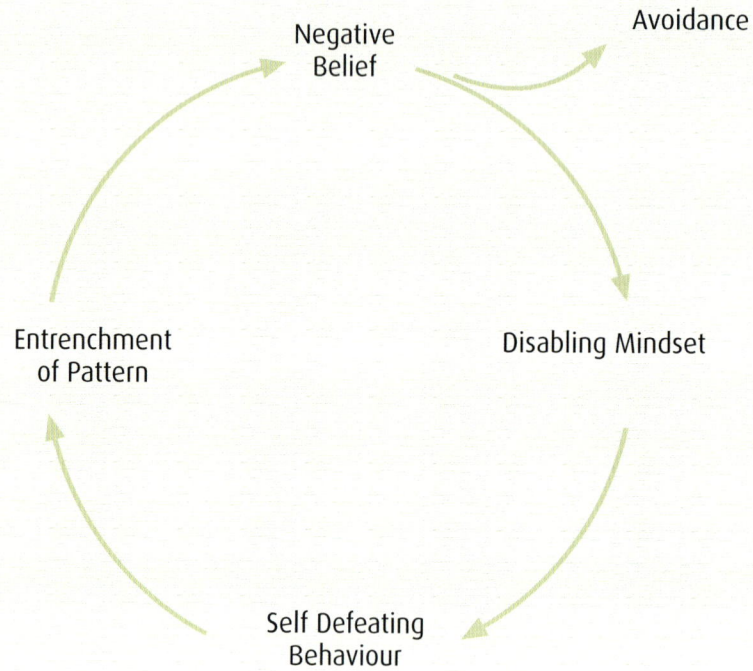

Negative Belief

Avoidance

Disabling Mindset

Self Defeating Behaviour

Entrenchment of Pattern

Examples of Negative Belief Cycles

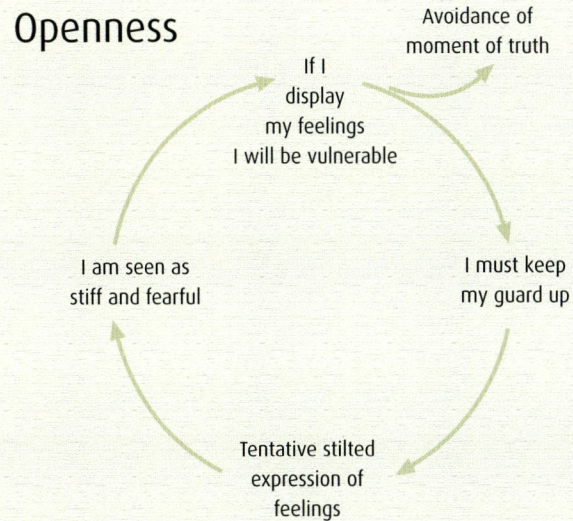

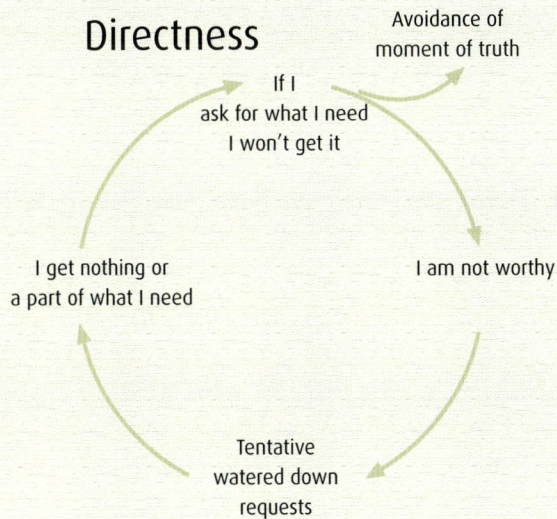

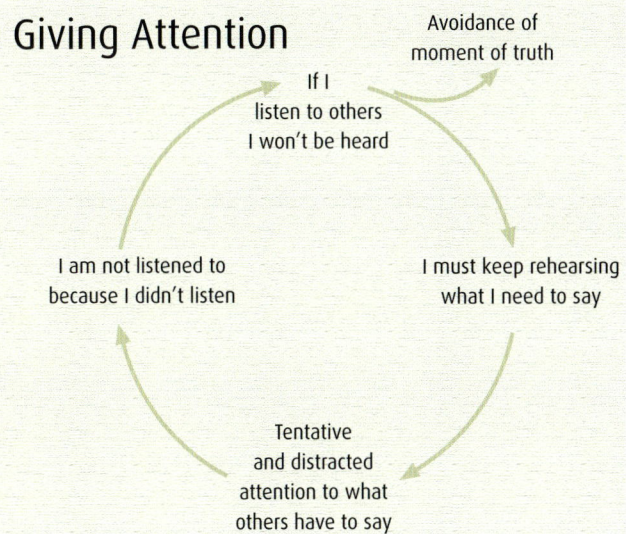

Conflict

If I disagree then I will lose the arguement
→ Avoidance of moment of truth
→ I can't win
→ Tentative fearful expression of slight concern
→ I am not taken seriously

Openness

If I display my feelings I will be vulnerable
→ Avoidance of moment of truth
→ I must keep my guard up
→ Tentative stilted expression of feelings
→ I am seen as stiff and fearful

Directness

If I ask for what I need I won't get it
→ Avoidance of moment of truth
→ I am not worthy
→ Tentative watered down requests
→ I get nothing or a part of what I need

Giving Attention

If I listen to others I won't be heard
→ Avoidance of moment of truth
→ I must keep rehearsing what I need to say
→ Tentative and distracted attention to what others have to say
→ I am not listened to because I didn't listen

The ways out of these block cycles are similar to those already discussed. Firstly, you can choose not to enter the cycle and feel the pressure. This will be sub-optional for any regenerative change cycle you are engaged in, as the cycle will not go away and change necessarily provokes pressure and stress. The other options are to prepare and rehearse different behaviour choices and to reframe the disabling mindsets. They are after all fantasies and replacing "I can't win" with "I always win" is just as far fetched but much more motivating.

Leaders have a tendency to treat themselves as single units of influence who only rely on their own strengths and feel uniquely responsible for what happens. The higher up an organisation the more lonely leaders often report themselves to be. This view makes it much more difficult to prepare for and triumph through those testing times that forge Leadership character and enable continued regeneration of their organisations. There is a responsibility for leaders to build a support and challenge network that contains complementary strengths. These networks must include bosses, peers and subordinates but should, critically, have potentially more objective contributions from outside a leader's immediate surrounding hierarchy where there is less likelihood of partisan agendas clouding judgement and help.

These contributors would include coaches, mentors, non executives and advisors from within and without the organisation. There is still a residual sense that using advisors shows weakness rather than not using them shows stupidity. In fact one of the defining competences of a senior leader is their capability at putting the appropriate advisory group together.

Always working in relationship will mean a leader has access to other strengths, diversity in innovation and productivity and the transforming courage which comes from knowing they are not on their own. Although the world can be said to change one individual at a time there also needs to be regular avalanches of group change for legacies to be achieved. The leader's capacity to utilise moments of truth as opportunities to regenerate rather than degenerate relies not just on their own resources, but also the resources of the teams they build around themselves.

FORUMS FOR CHANGE
Regenerative Teamworking

All the paradoxes and positive and negative elements found and needing resolution in organisations and individual leaders exist in the team's potential to be a regenerative force. At best a team resolves its Identity, Significance and Competence in tandem with individuals and the organisation. They all need to nest within each other and be aligned so that stakeholder needs can be met.

This nested regeneration spreads deeper and further. Working through the regeneration process enables organisations to differentiate themselves, to make themselves distinctive. The same is true of regenerative leaders and teams. The distinct organisation creates distinctive leaders, creates distinctive teams and vice-versa, all three feed off and into each other. The organisation, its leaders and teams influence stakeholders and the wider society and are in their turn influenced by the unfolding social political and economic context. It is possible to create a developmental golden thread or virtuous iterative cycle and to trace this from the leader, through the team, through stakeholders, through society and back to the individual leader. There will then be a sense of creating sustainable leaders creating sustainable teams, creating sustainable organisations creating a sustainable world. This cycle of regenerative leadership starts with the individual leader's action and reflection and needs the potency of a team committed to regeneration to move the organisation and the world forward in a connected and sustainable manner.

The Sustainable Gold Thread of Regeneration

Society

Stakeholders

Organisation

Teams

Leader

Teams used to be characterised as a select group of people coming together for a significant period of time with common purpose in order to reach shared objectives. This team provided a home base which the individual spent most of his time working in with infrequent, irregular forays into other special project teams.

Now an organisation's success can be measured by the capability of its people to work in a number of simultaneously operating teams with fluid membership often not meeting face to face or sharing a home base. This ability to cluster around what needs to be done, to join, to achieve and to move on in sequence and in parallel to the next or contemporaneous piece of work has become the hallmark of flourishing organisations.

It is now necessary for a number of types of team to configure and reconfigure and the form of each configuration, in terms of size, shape and duration of connection must follow the nature of the work to be done.

Teams, Squads and Communities within organisations necessarily construct themselves as matrices of responsibility and an individual's basic team consists of themselves and the person or people they are directly responsible to. This is usually one individual but can be a board or a committee. It is a solid reporting line and the people the line connects are the individual's basic team. Dotted line connections have become more numerous and it is not unusual for an individual to spend a lot or even all of their time and attention on work concerning the owner of the dotted line. These are basic "teams of two" and if they are not working well teamworking in its wider sense becomes problematic.

Building from these "teams of two" are the boss and peer based teams that are responsible for making organisations work. These primary work teams consist of a boss and the operational and functional members responsible for a discreet piece of operational activity and the creation of their future. Similarly there are primary work teams constructed along the dotted line matrices, for example, a regional marketing team, a global H.R. Team or a territory I.T. Support team, again with both an operational and innovative, creative agenda.

These primary teams are now less likely to spend time togethe, only meeting for operational review, for critical decision-making and short-term future planning. The opportunity for these primary work teams is that they become the nucleus of Regeneration activity, that they become the builders and the guardians of stakeholder legacy as well as the enablers of outputs and outcomes.

The primary team in reality is only the "team on the day", drawn from a squad which usually consists of the work team and their direct reports and functional specialists, as well as advisors from inside and outside the organisation appropriate to the task.

Most medium term, future design work and recovery or repair work, where breakdown has occurred, is done by teams configured from the wider community for which the primary team is responsible. These matrixed project teams have short to medium term life spans, tasked to deliver specific outputs which will then feed back in to the general planning and operating process of the organisation. This community needs to have a voice in the present and about the future, it is a dynamic entity, not just a supplier of units of output. Generally the community has and should feel that although it is in its own right a stakeholder of the work team, that it is responsible for and excited about and engaged with the delivery of stakeholder legacies.

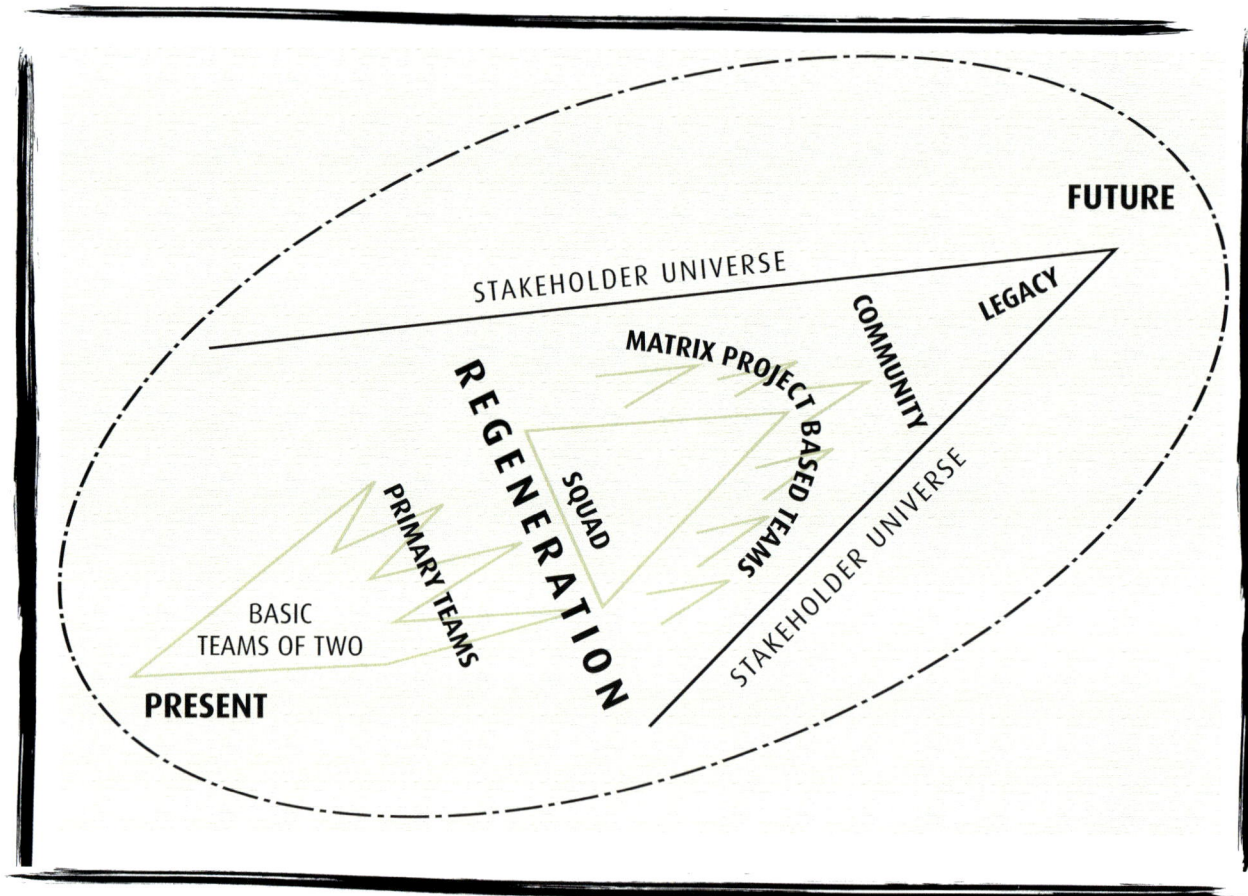

Types of Team

BASIC 'TEAMS OF TWO'

PRIMARY TEAM

SQUAD

MATRIX PROJECT TEAMS

COMMUNITY

STAKEHOLDERS

STAKEHOLDER

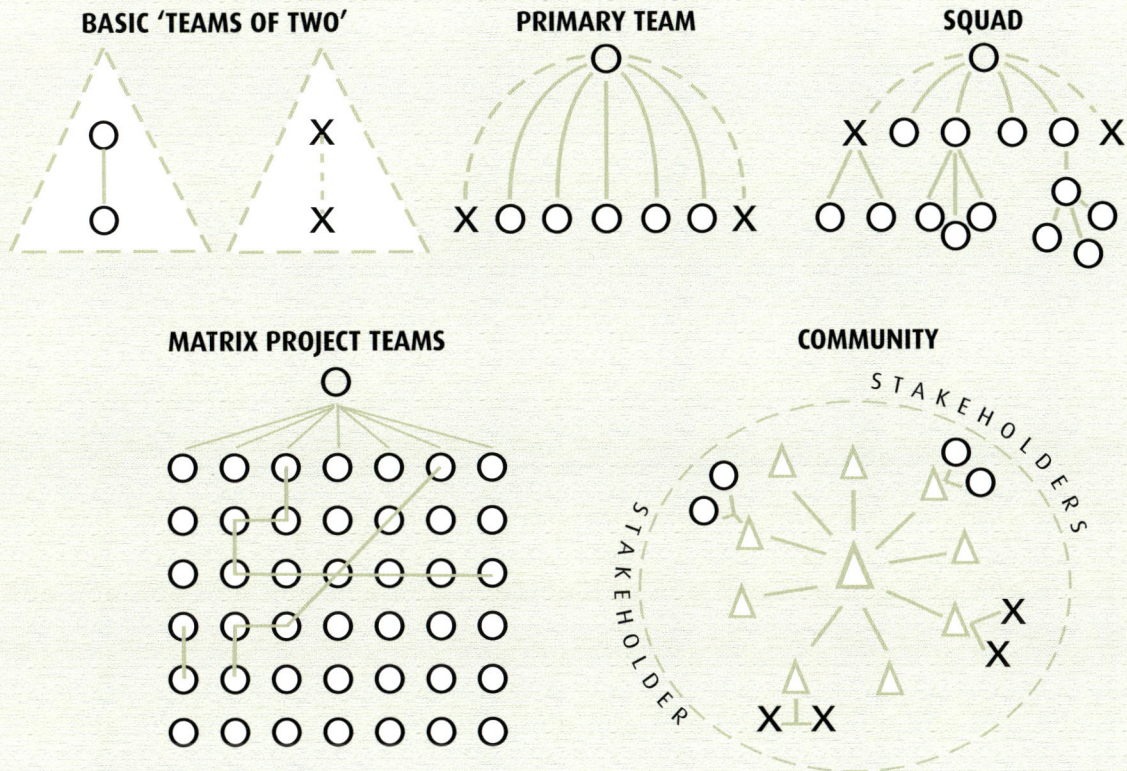

All these kinds of teams are in live orbit around each other constantly moving, impacting and influencing each other. They will all, to some degree, have a mixture of responsibility for operational maintenance activities and strategic delivery of outputs and outcomes over medium term time frames. What should keep them in useful orbit will be a co-created sense of Identity, Significance and Competence and a commitment to deliver the stakeholder legacies forged with and by them.

The rhythm with which these types of team interact and reconfigure is important as they not only need to influence each other but nest within each other's timeline and deliverables. Ensuring that all these types of team exist and have a healthy robust interdependent life in pursuit of stakeholder needs and, that they have the right degree of similarity and difference in their composition to be innovative is critical for regeneration to become embedded in an organisation's life and to provide stakeholder lift.

When leaders are creating the right forums for change, where the appropriate people, individually and in their various teams, are talking and listening to each other on an agenda designed to resolve needs and produce legacies, then the leaders are generating lift. By aligning the stakeholder's need with the leadership's aspiration and the individual and team's efforts to the creation of stakeholder legacy like two propeller blades spinning around the appropriate forums for change they will begin to spin and lift. Fusing these elements together into a single conversation with one direction and destination has the potential to accumulate enormous momentum. Provided the blades are joined by forums that truly facilitate co-creation then stakeholder and leadership needs become indissoluble and organisational individual and team activity lead inexorably to the creation of legacy.

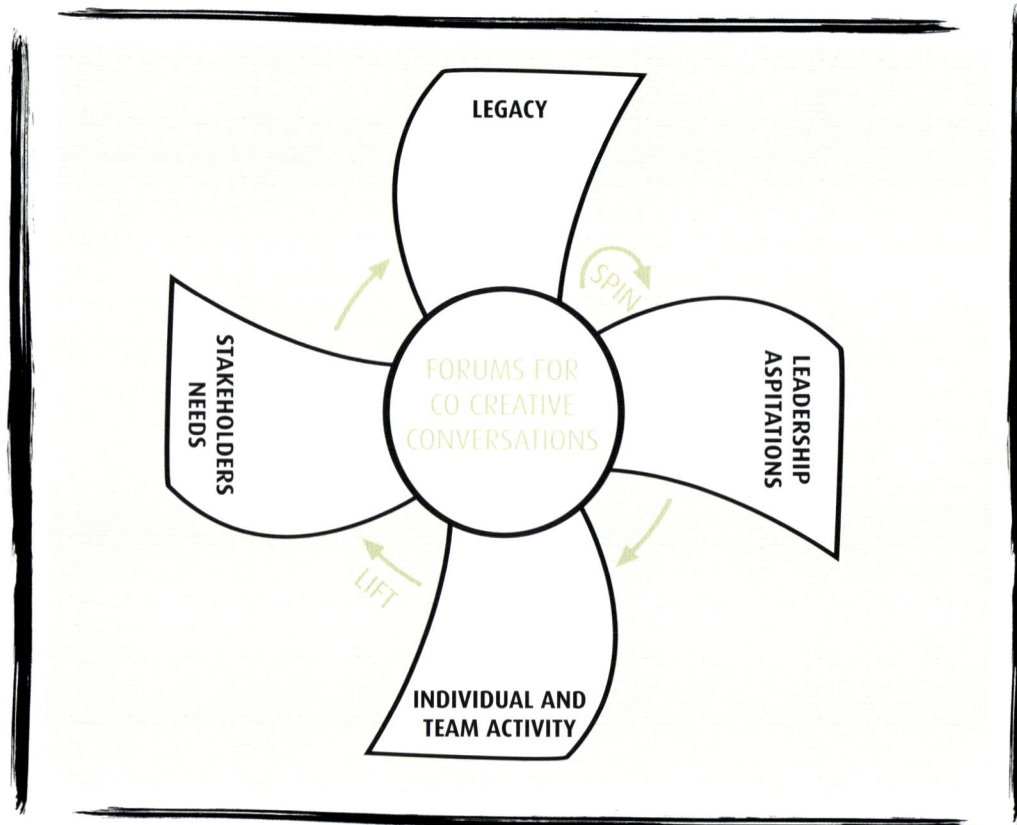

The Stakeholder Universe

Knowing and deciding who your stakeholders are can be a vexing question. It could be perceived that a country, an individual, an organisation or team only exists to meet their own needs, that there is no interdependence no reason to satisfy others in order to attain success. Every point of interaction is a war/competition with a clear winner and loser and resources are there to be exploited indiscriminately to the pursuit of self centered aggrandisement. This is the realm of the father of the people, the president for life, the robber baron, the monopolist, the divisional tyrant, the departmental dictator, the rapacious trader, the leader as master who sees stakeholders as targets to be squeezed of all of their worth and then marginalized into a subordinate position. Happily, because interdependence and transparency of interaction are increasing there is less possibility to perceive the world and behave in such a way. Unhappily megalomaniacs are still being born and bred.

The other extreme is to believe that everyone and everything has a vested interest in each entity's existence and that everything that a protagonist does must accommodate a sacred duty to accommodate all needs ultimately at the expense of their own. They seek out the smallest interdependencies and lavish them with disproportionate attention. This is the domain of the martyr, the saintly fool, the evangelist, the fellow traveller, the self appointed organisation conscience, the gung ho NGO, the departmental moral arbiter and the leader as servant. Happily as this extreme becomes more pragmatically mainstream then the loonier indulgences of the self indulgent diminish. Unhappily, sloppy sentimentality, the lush response to the small provocation is becoming public currency.

So, if you can't just please yourself and you can't hope to please everybody, what do you do?

Stakeholders will have relationship journeys of varying lengths and intensities therefore, differing interdependencies will be in the foreground or background of consciousness, depending on where they are in their relationship journey.

The primary interdependencies and therefore predominate stakeholders will be at least five constituencies:

- The customer and / or consumers whose needs the organisation exists to satisfy.
- The owners of the organisation.
- The suppliers who provide the inputs to enable added value to be generated.
- The leaders of the organisation and the people who work to add value in it and their families.
- The regulator who provides the "franchise to operate" or the organisation's "right to transact".

These groups will have, potentially, many sub groups with similar and distinctive needs of the same organisation. Some, such as the regulators, may have fairly constant needs over the medium term and others are more open to changes such as the consumer's driven need for continuously contemporary fashionable innovations.

Stakeholder Mapping

So a straightforward consumer map might look like this:

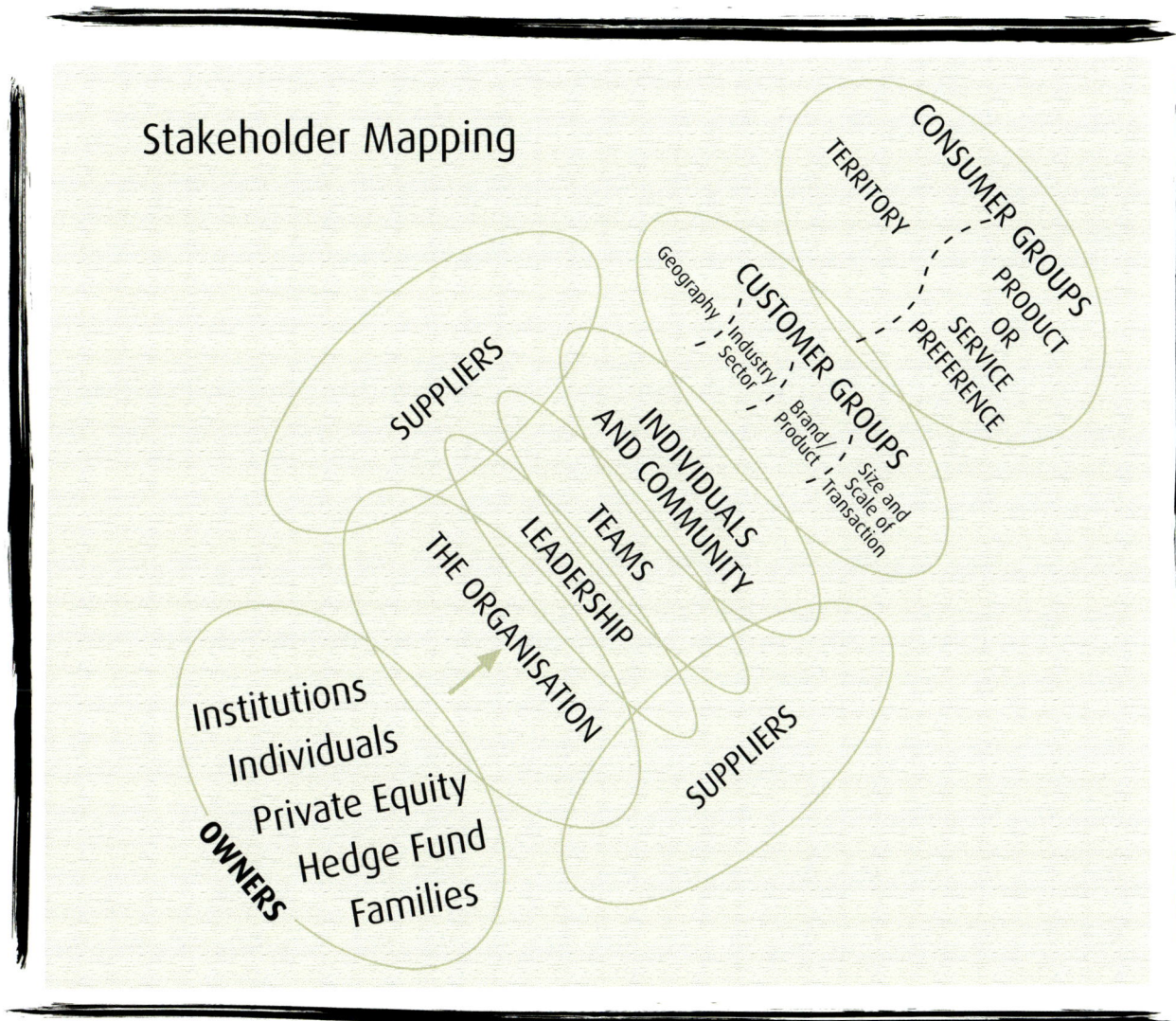

All the above groupings can be sliced into usefully differentiated relationships where different legacies are needed.

Of course, the complexity of the stakeholder universe will depend on the organisation's current context. During merger or takeover Merchant Banks and City Analysts may become prominent stakeholders. A move to a larger market might entail joining with a Third Party Logistics supplier. Social and political change may mean an NGO comes into the foreground of stakeholder interdependence.

For an organisation to engage productively with its stakeholder grouping it needs to judiciously map those groups it will need to engage with at a legacy level over its next regenerative cycle of say three to five years. As a prerequisite to this the leader and their teams have to have gone through a regenerative pause for themselves and the organisation they represent, rebasing and recalibrating their own Identity, Significance and Competence and formulating the legacy they want to bequeath to each other and the next generation of the organisation's leadership.

Once this base clarity is clear enough, it may be enhanced or changed by contact with other stakeholders, then it is possible to start to engage the chosen stakeholders in the process of co-creation of mutual legacies to determine what the groupings can uniquely do together that they can't do separately. From this will come a regeneration agenda which will need initiating work done by matrixed teams before becoming part of both stakeholders' mutual and separate planning processes. The regeneration agenda is likely to be diverse and complex, that is, a number of different co-created experiments coming at big problems and opportunities from various angles and complex in that if the issues were simple they would have been resolved or realised by one stakeholder without the need of a co-creation process. A good indication that regeneration is becoming embedded in stakeholder relationships is when regular joint co-creative planning sessions occur. These can range from relaxed yet rigourous monthly work life balance discussions over a family meal, to formal six monthly joint account planning workshops between a supplier and a customer or, regular top to top summits between the global leaders of a manufacturer and a retailer. All of these indicate that legacy co-creation and regeneration are beginning to become an innovative way of life rather than trauma driven, crisis meetings of last resort.

So regeneration is different. It is not a one way mechanical change process with a leader driving their own solutions through the organisation out to the stakeholders. It also isn't about replacing a number of existing organisational systems and processes (e.g. information, customer service, purchasing) in a hope that they will now be modern enough to keep their stakeholders happy. Finally it is not just about changing the culture of an organisation and remotivating and retraining its staff in isolation of the needs of its significant stakeholders. Regeneration is relational, focused on real jointly identified needs, co-created legacy aspirations and is achieved jointly with the stakeholders.

Regeneration is not just

STAKEHOLDERS

A top down heirarchical cascade

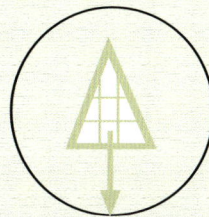

STAKEHOLDERS

New processes imposed on existing orgnisational systems

STAKEHOLDERS

Centrally controlled culture and behaviour change Programmes

Regeneration is

STAKEHOLDERS

Maximising stakeholder value through joint legacy and co-creation

REGENERATIVE GOVERNANCE

Organisational governance and regulation should be concerned with the long term protection of stakeholder interests, giving guidance to leaders on how they engage with present and future opportunities and challenges and, as a supervisor of performance and crisis recovery.

Whatever form governance takes, a minister representing a set of statute, an oversight committee, a chairman, a non executive board, non executive directors, auditors, industry regulators, watchdogs, institutional investors or rating agencies, they are stakeholders in the organisation's ongoing success and all of the organisation's other stakeholders have a vested interest in their good governance of the organisation.

All forms of governance, whether embodied in statutes, in protocol or in responsible groups and individuals, need to be always relevant to their present context so that they perform their responsibilities of protection, guidance and supervision in the manner 'of their time'. To do this each body needs to always be at their sparkling best. They have to be clear about their Identity, what values they hold, what they stand for and against; to have a clear view of the fundamental changes that need to occur for their industry sector or the organisations they oversee, so that they can always have a Significant future and to be clear about the range of Competence they need to express to discharge their duties to the highest level.

Governance can be seen as the mouthing of repetitive unchanging mantras or as a rubber stamp to executive action, rather than as a responsibility to ensure that an organisation engages in regenerative change cycles of Identity, Significance and Competence and is guided away from the degenerative change cycle of Anomie, Notoriety and Mediocrity.

To protect, guide and supervise success and crisis recovery effectively governance agencies need to ensure that organisations are regularly resetting, recalibrating and abiding by their commercial, social and ethical compass. This can include criticism of an organisation's strategic direction by a minority shareholder, a tribunal intervening in exploitative employment practices, an auditor refusing to sign a set of accounts or a prosecutor bringing legal action for fraud. All of these actions can be an invitation to regeneration, the rebasing of an organisation so that it is once again on a regenerative path not just a return to current normal operating. Rather than waiting for some crisis to alert them to danger it is beneficial for governance agencies to see their job as ensuring that regenerative change cycles are embedded in the organisations they oversee, to ensure there is a long range legacy perspective taken and that stakeholder needs are the forces for action rather than the personal agendas of the leadership group.

The other fundamental proactive area for oversight is the creation and maintenance of the relationship journey web. Are there mechanisms in place for ensuring that appropriate joining, achieving and moving on phases and programs are in place so that the organisation has the necessary difference and oxygen needed to keep the innovative blood flow moving around the system ensuring its ongoing health. Interventions here can range from a shareholder insisting that an organisation be open to take over (joining), a non executive director challenging what they see as unambitious targets (achieving) or a chairman insisting that a successful chief executive leave (move on) to their next level of accomplishment.

Legacy based prophecy and a generational timeline of success also gives Remuneration Committees the opportunity to reward organisation's leaders for fundamentally changing their organisation's landscapes to ensure stakeholder success.

Regenerative governance is proactive rather than just reactive, it does mean oversight groups need to look to their own regeneration in order to be better able to pursue their work. It gives a map of the fundamental elements, whose existence they can be responsible for, that enable organisations to flourish for generations and it moves the focus away from either just complaining or clearing up the mess.

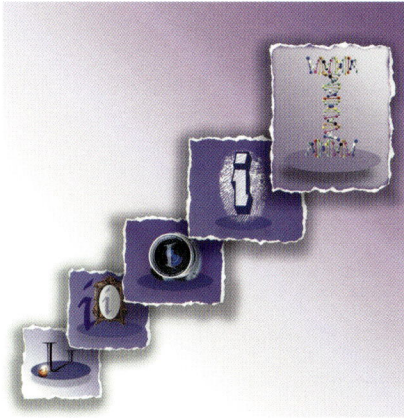

IN CONCLUSION

Organisations are hot houses, sublime opportunities for both construction or destruction for regeneration or degeneration. Individuals bring all of themselves, the useful and less useful, their talents and their idiosyncratic set of normal neurosis, these can be harnessed for torment and failure, or success and fulfilment.

Regeneration and co-creation gives a framework for ensuring that individuals and organisations move on to their next positive hybrid state so that they are always relevant, slightly ahead of their time and do what they are supposed to do, meet their stakeholder needs and enjoy their lives. This means ensuring that the conditions exist for them to experience the peaks embodied in the intimate connections of joining, the adrenalin rushes of achieving and the deep sense of completion when they fully move on in their relationship journey.

Thank yous

An enormous thank you to Karen Mortimore for bringing the design elements of the book bursting to life, to Simon Knibbs for polishing the images for public consumption and to Stephanie Szakalo for her management of the publishing and printing of the book.
Without you three this would have been a much lonelier endeavour.

Many people have, over the years, helped to shape the views expressed in this book.
I especially want to thank Pam Roderick for being a constant support, co-creator of great regeneration events and co-conspirator in the art of useful living. Ralf Schneider for the most stimulating discussions, warming debates and great opportunities to do life changing work.
Ed Smith for shaping and trusting my thinking and the opportunity to let the Relationship Journey and Cycles of Experience play out on a major stage. Robert Leechman for his wise and pragmatic views. Gareth M. Davies and Richard Burns for excitement and energy in creating the early skeleton of regeneration. Irial Finan and Warwick White for the initial trust and interest in Legacy based strategy.

Finally, thank you to Charlotte Hampton for being able to read this technophobe's pencilled scrawl and produce a sparkling manuscript.

* The origins of this image were co-created by the executive board of Citic Prudential PRC.

Also to istockphoto.com